The World of Animals

*by the same author*

The Biology of Art
The Mammals
Men and Snakes (co-author)
Men and Apes (co-author)
Men and Pandas (co-author)
Zootime
Primate Ethology (editor)
The Naked Ape
The Human Zoo
Patterns of Reproductive Behaviour
Intimate Behaviour
Manwatching
Gestures (co-author)
Animal Days
The Soccer Tribe
Inrock
The Book of Ages
The Art of Ancient Cyprus
Bodywatching
The Illustrated Naked Ape
Dogwatching
Catwatching
The Secret Surrealist
Catlore
The Animals Roadshow
The Human Nestbuilders
Horsewatching
The Animal Contract
Animalwatching
Babywatching
Christmaswatching

# THE WORLD OF
# ANIMALS

## Desmond Morris

with illustrations by
Peter Barrett

VIKING

*VIKING*

*Published by the Penguin Group*

*Penguin Books USA Inc., 375 Hudson Street, New York, New York 10014, U.S.A.*
*Penguin Books Ltd, 27 Wrights Lane, London W8 5TZ, England*
*Penguin Books Australia Ltd, Ringwood, Victoria, Australia*
*Penguin Books Canada Ltd, 10 Alcorn Avenue, Toronto, Ontario, Canada M4V 3B2*
*Penguin Books (N.Z.) Ltd, 182–190 Wairau Road, Auckland 10, New Zealand*

*Penguin Books Ltd, Registered Offices: Harmondsworth, Middlesex, England*

*First published in Great Britain by Jonathan Cape Limited, 1993*
*First published in the United States of America by Viking,*
*a division of Penguin Books USA Inc., 1993*

*1 3 5 7 9 10 8 6 4 2*

*Text copyright © Desmond Morris, 1993*
*Illustrations copyright © Peter Barrett, 1993*
*All rights reserved*

*Library of Congress Catalog Card Number: 93–60092*

*ISBN 0-670-85184-1*

*Printed and bound in Great Britain by*
*Butler & Tanner Ltd, Frome and London*
*Set in Garamond 3*

# Contents

INTRODUCTION . . . . . . . . . . . . . . 6

THE ELEPHANT . . . . . . . . . . . . . 9

THE GORILLA . . . . . . . . . . . . . 13

THE KOALA . . . . . . . . . . . . . . 19

THE WHALE . . . . . . . . . . . . . . 23

THE LION . . . . . . . . . . . . . . . 29

THE BISON . . . . . . . . . . . . . . 33

THE GIRAFFE . . . . . . . . . . . . . 37

THE WOLF . . . . . . . . . . . . . . . 43

THE HIPPO . . . . . . . . . . . . . . 49

THE CHEETAH . . . . . . . . . . . . . 53

THE SEA LION . . . . . . . . . . . . . 57

THE ZEBRA . . . . . . . . . . . . . . 61

THE CAMEL . . . . . . . . . . . . . . 67

THE CHIMPANZEE . . . . . . . . . . . 71

THE ARMADILLO . . . . . . . . . . . . 77

THE PLATYPUS . . . . . . . . . . . . . 81

THE TIGER . . . . . . . . . . . . . . 87

THE BEAVER . . . . . . . . . . . . . . 93

THE RHINO . . . . . . . . . . . . . . 99

THE BUSH BABY . . . . . . . . . . . . 105

THE BEAR . . . . . . . . . . . . . . . 109

THE DOLPHIN . . . . . . . . . . . . . 115

THE KANGAROO . . . . . . . . . . . . 119

THE PANDA . . . . . . . . . . . . . . 125

# Introduction

WHY DOES A BEAVER BUILD A DAM? WHY DOES A ZEBRA HAVE STRIPES? How does a camel go without water? Why does a hippo wag its tail? Which animal sings the longest song? What happens to lion cubs when their father dies? How do pandas survive in the bamboo forests?

The world of animals is full of surprising discoveries. Some people imagine that we know all the answers and that there is little more to be learned. How wrong they are. The truth is that there are still many animal mysteries to solve. Every year new facts come to light, giving us a clearer picture of the strange and wonderful creatures with which we share this small planet.

Every animal alive on the Earth today has found its own special solution to the problem of survival. For zoologists each animal is a challenge. We want to uncover the secrets of how it manages to succeed in a highly competitive world.

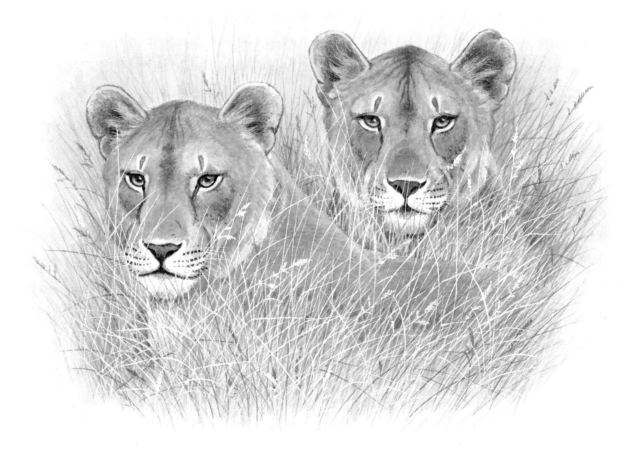

Whenever we encounter a new animal, there are a hundred questions to ask. This is true even with the most famous of animals – the ones we have met many times before, in pictures, on television, or at the zoo.

We all have ideas about these animal "stars," but they are often based on fiction rather than fact. There are too many romantic tales about animals that have little to do with their real lives. They are reduced to cartoon characters, as if they are funny versions of us. A certain animal is "savage," "cruel," "creepy," "silly," "pretty," or "sad," because its face reminds us of people who are like this. But these labels usually have nothing to do with the true animal. If we wish to understand them properly, we have to look at animals afresh, with open minds.

How does each animal find its food and how does it avoid becoming a tasty meal for somebody else? Where does it sleep? Does it have a nest or a den of some kind? How does it fight, mate and rear its young? How friendly is it? Does it live in a big group, small family or on its own?

If we want to get closer to animals we must try to see the world from their point of view. The trick is to stop thinking of ourselves as superior to them. If we look down on animals we have no hope of understanding them. We must go out and study them on their own terms.

This is what more and more naturalists are doing today. They spend long hours, weeks and even years, sitting in the natural homes of the animals, quietly watching and making notes of what they see. They do not need any special equipment to do this, just a pair of eyes to see the actions and a pair of ears to hear the sounds. Those, and a pen and paper, are all that is necessary to start a new project. And there are thousands of animals out there that have never been studied, just waiting for someone with enough patience to investigate them.

What this book does is to take some of the most familiar and famous of all animals and look at them carefully, one by one. In each case I have painted a portrait in words to match the pictures made by Peter Barrett. Just as he has tried to show the animals exactly as they are, without any exaggerations, so I have tried to record the special way in which each one lives, without distorting the facts.

If, when you have read these pages, you feel the urge to go out and study an animal yourself, then I shall be well satisfied and I am sure you will never regret it.

Desmond Morris
Oxford, 1992

# The Elephant

THE ELEPHANT'S MOST AMAZING FEATURE IS ITS TRUNK. IF YOU CAN IMAGINE having the end of your nose and your upper lip pulled further and further away from your face, that will give you some idea of how the elephant's trunk was formed over millions of years. As it grew longer, it became stronger. Today it contains no fewer than sixty thousand muscles and the elephant uses its trunk in many different ways.

Its main job is to stretch out and pick the grasses, leaves, shoots, twigs and fruits on which the animal feeds. The end of the trunk curls around the food object, grips it tight, plucks it and then carries it to the open mouth. This action is repeated endlessly, time after time, day after day. For the elephant, feeding takes up at least eighteen hours out of every twenty-four.

The trunk is also used for drinking. The animal sucks about 2 gallons of water up into it, closes the tip and then pushes it into the mouth. There it squirts the liquid straight down its throat. If the water supply is good, an adult elephant will drink between 35 and 58 gallons of water a day. When water is short, the trunk is used to sniff the ground in search of hidden water lying deep below the surface. If it finds a promising spot, the animal then digs with its huge tusks until it has made a hole deep enough to suck out a little liquid.

The tusks, which are also used for stripping bark from trees, are two upper teeth that have become bigger and bigger and longer and longer until they are now massive tools for feeding and fighting. The largest tusk ever seen was nearly 11.5 feet long, but tusks as big as that are rare. Usually they only grow to about half that length. When the elephant is trying to move a heavy object, such as a log, it combines its tusks and its trunk and puts itself to work like a fork-lift truck.

The trunk is also used during bathing. Elephants have to keep their nearly one-inch-thick skin in good condition and like to bathe every day. When they do so, they squirt water over their backs. In very hot weather this also keeps them cool. If they are in a mud wallow, they use the trunk to spray liquid mud over their skin. This dries like a mud-pack and helps to kill skin-pests and protect the surface of the animal. If the earth is very dry, the trunk is used to scatter dust over the skin, during bouts of dust-bathing.

Surprisingly, elephants are good swimmers and when they are in deep water they use their trunks like snorkels, holding them up high in the air. They also raise them high when they are on dry land if they smell something exciting. Turning the tip this way and that they can quickly tell which way the smell is coming from. If it means danger, they can then take action before the threat has come too close.

Because the trunk is a super-nose, elephants can use it to sniff anything they touch, learning a great deal about the object as they do so. It is fascinating to watch

such a huge beast delicately sniffing a small flower, or brushing the end of its trunk gently over the face of one of its companions.

The trunk caresses other elephants during courtship and when friends are greeting one another. Mothers can examine their babies by feeling them all over with the sensitive tip of the trunk. Rival elephants sometimes wrestle with their trunks when they fight one another.

When they are alarmed, elephants employ their trunks in yet another way – as trumpets. When they scream through their long "noses," the hollow tubes inside turn the trunk into a musical wind instrument.

So the elephant's trunk is a delicate nose, a sensitive lip, a firm hand, a strong arm, a powerful hosepipe, a snorkel and a loud trumpet, all in one. It is one of the most extraordinary organs in the entire animal world.

Although we may marvel at the elephant's trunk and its many uses, the animal's main claim to fame has to be its huge size. Elephants are the largest land animals on earth. A big male can weigh up to 13,000 pounds and when it is born a baby elephant is heavier than a fully grown man.

Being so enormous helps the elephants in two ways. It makes it possible for them to reach high up in the trees when searching for food. It also makes it very difficult for any killers, such as lions, tigers or wild dogs, to attack them. Only a newborn baby elephant could fall prey to hunting animals, and even then there is little chance of an attack succeeding because the adult elephants stand guard over the new arrival and protect it from any harm.

A female elephant is pregnant for nearly two years, the longest pregnancy in the whole world of animals. When the baby is born, the mother is helped by her female friends. These act as midwives, clustering round the newborn, cleaning it, helping it to its feet and shielding it from any lurking dangers. It would be a brave killer that would risk coming close to a group of females at this time.

Adult female elephants live in a close group and always move about together. The group is made up of several sisters, their young ones and probably an old grandmother elephant. This grandmother is the leader and ruler of the group. If there is a hint of danger – an unusual smell or a strange, unexpected movement in the distance – it is she who faces it, while the others form a tight cluster around the calves. Because she is the biggest of the females and because she shows such courage when defending her little herd, the big game hunters who went elephant-shooting in Victorian times thought she must be the bull elephant. In those days they were so used to the idea of the male as the head of the family, they could not believe that a female could be the boss.

Years later, when people started studying wild elephants more carefully, they discovered that the bulls live alone, outside the family group. They are even bigger than the female group-leader. In a one-to-one fight, a big bull could easily defeat a big cow, and could then move in and become the herd boss. But it is not that easy because, if he tried to do so, the females would get together and gang up on him. For female elephants the golden rule is "strength in numbers."

The males are only allowed into the herd when the females are ready to mate. Afterwards they must leave and return to their solo lifestyle. Sometimes a few males may live together in a loose herd, but this does not last very long and they do not help one another like the females.

After it is born the young elephant grows very fast. It feeds on its mother's milk for over three years, sucking the liquid not with its trunk but with its mouth. Once it is weaned it will never again take food directly into its mouth in this way. It will always use its trunk first and then transfer the food to its mouth.

By the time it is six years old the young elephant will weigh ten times as much as it did at birth. Four years later it will start breeding itself. If it is a female it will produce a new calf every three years until it dies or is too old to breed. A few elephants manage to live almost as long as man, but most will be lucky to get past thirty years of age.

There is a romantic story that, when they are about to die, elephants shuffle off to a special, sacred place called "the elephants' graveyard." The legend began because explorers sometimes came across big collections of elephant bones all lying together on the ground. The truth about these graveyards, and it is a sad truth, is that they are places where whole herds of animals were slaughtered by human hunters and their bodies left to rot. The unromantic fact is that when an elephant dies it drops dead on the spot, wherever it happens to be.

Recently, all too many of them have been dropping on the spot. In Africa, just over ten years ago, there were over a million elephants. Since then poachers have killed half of them. All that these men wanted was the ivory. The rest of the dead elephant was left untouched where it fell. They stole the great curved tusks and smuggled them to the Far East where carvers shaped them into expensive ornaments. The ivory traders grew rich, caring little for the fate of the elephants just so long as there were more in Africa waiting to be killed.

Eventually the numbers fell so low that a world ban on the sale of ivory was agreed. This helped a little, but the more daring poachers still attacked at night and continued to rob Africa of its greatest animal.

With the Asian elephant, mass slaughter is not possible because there are already so few animals left. At the last count it was found that less than 50,000 remained in the entire continent. They survive in small, remote areas of the forests of India and Sri Lanka, through Indochina, Malaysia and southern China, down into parts of Indonesia.

The Asian and the African are the only two kinds of elephants left alive today. They are very similar, but differ in several details. The Asian has a domed forehead; the African's is flat. The Asian carries its head low and has a humped back; the African carries its head higher and has a slight dip in the middle of its back. The ears of the Asian elephant are smaller than those of the African. (This is because an elephant's ears are used for cooling the body, and the African suffers more from the heat than the Asian.) The tusks of the female Asian elephant are so small they cannot be seen outside its mouth; the tusks of the female African elephant, although smaller than those of the male, are clearly visible at a distance. The Asian elephant is slightly smaller than the African and it is also easier to tame. Asian elephants have been used from ancient times for clearing forests, for ceremonial parades, for warfare, as beasts of burden and as circus performers. Being much more difficult to control, the African elephant has been spared these insulting tasks.

By the time you read these words, you can be certain of one thing – there will already be far fewer elephants in the world. After millions of years, the era of these animal giants is drawing to a close. We have been very lucky to be alive while they are still with us, to marvel at them and enjoy their company.

# The Gorilla

OF ALL THE MONKEYS AND APES ALIVE TODAY, THE GORILLA IS THE BIGGEST and strongest. When explorers first discovered it, deep inside the tropical forests of West Africa, they were terrified. Its huge arms, its massive body, its powerful jaws and its fierce expression frightened them so much that their only thought was how quickly they could kill the monster.

When they started firing their guns and the great male gorillas saw their families wounded and screaming in pain, the explorers had good reason to be afraid. Driven wild with fury, the great males charged their tormentors, roaring their anger. When this happened, according to early travelers' tales, the gorillas would crush the barrels of the guns between their teeth and then tear limb from limb any of the humans they could catch.

Those travelers that managed to escape and return home brought with them horrific tales of brutal, enraged giants thirsting for human blood. Their audiences believed every word and before very long the gorilla was labelled as a vicious, violent monster.

This picture of the animal was to last for a hundred years, until just over thirty years ago, when zoologists first ventured into gorilla country to make a careful study of their everyday life. Armed only with cameras and notebooks, these scientists sat for hour after hour, just watching quietly. When the family of gorillas moved on, they followed at a distance. They tried never to let the animals out of their sight. In this way they were able to keep a "gorilla diary" and to build up an entirely new picture of these gigantic animals.

What are the gorillas really like? The biggest shock came when it was realized that they are not, in fact, very aggressive, but very shy. If you leave them in peace, they leave you in peace. The idea that they are always on the lookout for someone to tear to pieces is complete nonsense. Only if you attack the gorilla family, will the big male become aggressive. His actions are always a defence against attack. He never starts the trouble, as the early hunters suggested. In other words, it is the humans who are the brutal ones, not the gorillas.

Today it is possible to go on a gorilla-watching safari. Thousands of tourists every year enjoy the thrill of trekking through the forests until they find a family of the great apes. Once there, they sit nearby and study them. They can photograph them and watch them in this way for hours on end, and not a single tourist has ever been attacked or wounded. The gorillas see them but ignore them.

The truth is that gorillas, despite their fierce-looking faces, are gentle leaf-eaters. Their ancestors switched to leaf-eating and stem-chewing as a way of life millions of years ago. As time passed, these animals grew bigger and bigger. Today a male gorilla weighs twice as much as a male chimpanzee.

The problem with eating leaves and stems is they provide only very poor quality food. So leaf-eaters have to swallow large quantities of vegetation every day, just to survive. Out of every twelve daylight hours, gorillas must spend six hours picking and munching their food. Feeding rules their lives and even shapes their bodies.

They need bigger teeth to break open the tough stems and to grind up the leaves. The bigger teeth need larger jaws to hold them. The larger jaws need stronger muscles to open and shut them. And the larger muscles need heavy bones for attachment. This is why the gorilla looks so fierce. It has to have a massive head to enable it to feed. It has to wear a bony "crash-helmet," not for fighting but for chewing. The high crest of bone on top of the head is the anchor for the huge jaw muscles – muscles that, day after day, hardly stop working.

Gorillas move about far less than chimpanzees. A family group will on average travel only about half a mile a day. Again, this is connected with their special feeding habits. The smaller chimps prefer to eat ripe fruits, nuts and berries. To find these they have to keep searching, far and wide. The larger gorillas, seeking only leaves and stems, can find their food everywhere, without difficulty. It is all around them. They pick the best, then move on a little and start lazily browsing once more. It is a quiet life and a remarkably peaceful one.

They sleep wherever they find themselves at the end of the day. Being so huge – the males are over 5 feet tall and weigh 400 pounds – they do not take to the trees like their smaller cousins. Instead they build beds of leaves and twigs for themselves down at ground level. Babies sleep with their mothers.

In the morning they abandon their nests and do not return to them. When evening comes again, another set of beds will be made somewhere else. There is a special advantage in this. If they used the same nests night after night they might soon suffer from pests that would be able to stay put inside their "mattresses." So moving on each day helps to keep them clean and healthy.

Their great size, which forces them to live their lives down on the ground, also happily makes them too powerful for most of the killers that lurk in the forest. A leopard or a giant python would find an adult gorilla an impossible opponent. Only the very young animals could be attacked, and they are always under the watchful eye of their parents. Occasionally the little ones may take to the branches for bouts of acrobatic play, while their parents have a midday snooze, but even when this happens they never stray too far from the protection of the family group.

Baby gorillas are helpless when they are born and have to be carried by their mothers. They are not able to crawl until they are in their third month. They grow slowly and are not weaned until they are at least three years old. Because the females do not mate again until they have stopped feeding their infants, they therefore only breed once every four years.

When they can fend for themselves, the young gorillas leave the family group and strike off on their own. This applies to both young males and young females, which is uncommon. Usually, with animals that live in social groups, only the young males depart, the females staying in their family group even when they are adult.

The departure of the youngsters is not forced upon them. With some animals, the leader of the group drives the young males away when they are nearly adult, but this is not the case with gorillas. This is another example of the remarkably peaceful nature of gorilla family life.

A typical family group of gorillas consists of one big male, several adult females and five or six young ones. The male is called a "silverback" because once he has taken charge of a group he changes color. His back becomes silver-grey, as if he is wearing a pale saddle. This marks him out from the rest, who are black all over.

His small "harem" of females, usually only three or four, will have come from different family groups and are unrelated. As a result they pay little attention to one another. They are only interested in their babies and the big male. When the group is resting and there is a great deal of grooming going on, the females will hardly ever groom one another, spending all their grooming-time with their young or with the silverback.

Once more, this makes for a peaceful way of life, because there are no "junior wives" to be kept in order by "senior wives," as so often happens in the harems of other animals. Instead each female has her own respected position and together they share the favors of the silverback male.

Almost the only fighting that takes place in the world of the gorilla is that between a silverback male in charge of a family group and another male who challenges him for it. This is a rare event, but when it does occur, the whole forest shakes.

The males' threat displays consist of beating their chests, rushing sideways through the undergrowth, rearing up on their hind legs, ripping up plants, scattering vegetation, and making a great din, roaring, hooting and barking. From these displays it is nearly always possible for the two rivals to decide which one is the stronger. The weaker one then usually leaves without any blood being spilled.

Gorillas are so immensely powerful that even the smallest physical contact could easily wound both contestants so badly that neither would survive. With visual displays and loud noises they can settle their disputes without either of them suffering from injuries that could kill them.

Despite their great strength and their shy, retiring lifestyle, there are not many gorillas left alive today. There are two kinds: the short-haired lowland gorilla and the shaggy-haired mountain gorilla. It is thought that altogether there are now only about 13,000 of them left in Africa. Nearly all of them are lowland gorillas. Of the wonderful mountain gorillas, only a few hundred remain.

Everywhere the forests of these magnificent animals are being destroyed. The trees are taken for timber and the land is turned over to agriculture. Whole areas have been cleared for cattle and for crops.

In another twenty-three years the human population of West Africa will have doubled. With this increase, the need for farming land will become even more acute. The gorillas, one of our closest animal relatives, will find it hard to survive. The big males will beat their chests and roar their defiance, but like King Kong they will have no defence against bullets. Unless we can find some way to help them, there will soon be a sad end to one of the most awesome animals on earth – the mighty gorilla.

# The Koala

WITH ITS SOFT, FLUFFY FUR, ITS ROUNDED BODY AND ITS BIG, BUTTON nose, the Australian koala looks like the perfect pet. Its flat face and its cuddly appearance give it instant appeal. Everybody who meets one for the first time wants to hold it and fondle it. But, despite its looks, it is not at all suitable as a companion for humans.

It may appear to be a teddy bear come to life, but in reality it is a delicate and difficult animal to keep alive in captivity. This is because it feeds only on the leaves of just a few of the many species of Australian gum trees. Unless it gets exactly the right diet it soon curls up and dies.

Because it eats only oily leaves that have very little food value – and which would be poisonous to most other animals – it has very little energy to spare and must spend most of its time sleeping. It slumbers for no less than eighteen hours out of every twenty-four, more than twice as much as human beings.

It snoozes all through the daylight hours and hardly moves at all until the evening. Then it starts munching away on its tough oily leaves, grinding them up as finely as possible to make it easier to digest them. It goes on, picking and munching, picking and munching, until it has devoured about a pound of leaves and then settles itself down in the fork of a tree and drops off to sleep once more. That just about sums up its typical day.

Playful, intelligent, inquisitive, athletic . . . it is none of these things. In truth, it probably has the dullest and most sluggish lifestyle of any known mammal. As a companion animal it would soon become boring.

The only time that koalas show any sign of energetic movement is during the breeding season. This is in the summer, which in Australia means between October and February. It is then that the males set off at dusk, searching through the trees for females.

Both males and females have their own, specially defended territories, and normally they keep apart from one another. But when the breeding time arrives, the males are allowed into the females' home regions without any resistance.

These koala males become very noisy when they are searching for mates. They call out all night, making a terrible din. The sound they produce has been described as a growling bellow. Females, if they are alarmed or are being worried by the males, may give vent to a long wailing sound.

Although both males and females become adult when they are only two years old, the males cannot usually mate with females until they have reached the ripe old age of four. This delay is caused by the presence of other, more senior males, who refuse to allow the new males near the females. Only when they are big enough and strong enough to defend themselves and stand their ground against the older ones, can the young males hope to find a mate.

Koalas do not form pairs. There is no reason for the male and female to stay together after mating, because the female can easily rear her baby by herself and does not need any paternal help. So, after the male has traveled around the nearby territories and mated with as many females as he can find, he is free to return to his own personal tree-space and take up, once again, his quiet life of dozing and leaf-eating.

The territory of the male is about three times as big as that of the female. This means that, if a male wanders off around the edge of his personal space, he will come into contact with several females, one after the other. Each time he does so he mates quickly and then moves on, giving himself the best chance of increasing his number of offspring.

There is only one baby born each year to each female. Like the babies of so many pouched animals, it is tiny at birth. Less than an inch long, it weighs around a hundredth of an ounce, which is the same weight as an office paper-clip. If you hold a paper-clip in your hand you will get some idea of just how minute the koala baby really is.

There is a pouch on the front of the mother's body and the baby crawls into it when it is born. As soon as it struggles inside it attaches itself to one of the two long nipples there. Once in a while a koala gives birth to twins, and then both nipples are used.

A strange feature of the koala pouch is that it faces backwards. Instead of having the opening at the top, like a kangaroo, it is at the bottom, facing towards the mother's hind legs. For an animal that spends nearly all its time clambering around in the trees, this seems a very odd way of protecting its baby. A sudden jerk, or a fall, and one would imagine that the baby – especially when it is bigger – could drop out of the pouch entrance and down to the ground. Other tree-living pouched animals, like opossums, have the entrance at the top, where one would expect it to be, so the koala design is something of a puzzle. Perhaps it is a very strong pouch, stretched like elastic, that keeps the baby inside by holding it tight against its mother's body. This is a mystery we have yet to solve.

After a few months, the baby may leave the pouch for a little while, but soon rushes back to the security of its little pocket "den." But by the age of seven to eight months it has grown so big that it leaves the pouch for the final time, and makes no attempt to return. It still remains close to its mother, though, and spends a great deal of its time riding on her back. This continues until the end of its first year, when it leaves her in peace at last and begins to fend for itself.

Helping it now, as it explores the trees, are its very sharp, curved claws. It uses these to climb branches in search of fresh leaves and suitable resting places. On its front feet, these claws are arranged in an unusual way. Instead of having one thumb, grasping across at four fingers, as we do, it has two "thumbs" and only three "fingers" on each hand. The two thumbs grasp one side of a branch, while the three fingers grasp the other side, giving the animal an extremely powerful climbing grip. This also makes it difficult for an enemy to dislodge a koala, once it has clasped on to a bush or a tree. Its hands are like powerful clamps, encircling the wood.

Koalas were once very common all over Australia but, in the last century, new fashions began for the wearing of animal furs and millions of these small, inoffensive creatures were killed for their skins. On top of that, the new farming styles that Europeans took to Australia meant that huge fires burned out whole tracts of forest. Down on the ground some of the animals that lived there could save themselves by hiding in their burrows. Others could flee on fast legs and escape by running beyond the flames. But the little koalas, always so keen to stay up in the trees, found themselves stranded. As the fire swept though the tree-tops, they were engulfed and were killed instantly.

As if this were not enough, koalas are also vulnerable to disease. Many of them have been found to be suffering from serious illnesses, including a nasty fungus

infection that nearly always kills them. This disease also attacks humans, which means that cuddling koalas in wildlife parks is much more risky than most people realize.

By the middle of this century, the koala was thought to be on the road to extinction. There did not seem to be any way of saving it. But then Australians decided it was time to protect this immensely popular creature. They demanded that the killing should stop, and scientists began to study the health problems of the animal. The koala was saved. Today their numbers are on the increase again and it is now possible for many people to visit them in their natural home and watch them sitting snugly in their favorite trees.

Staying in the trees as a way of life may not help the koalas to avoid the forest fires, but it does have one great advantage. It means that they never have to worry about earthbound, prowling killers. A number of other pouched animals in Australia that do live on the ground have been killed in large numbers by the dogs that human settlers have brought with them to this continent. From this threat, at least, the koalas have little to fear.

Because it hardly ever climbs down to ground level, the koala cannot enjoy a regular drink at a stream or water-hole. Only when the weather becomes impossibly hot, does it venture from the trees to quench its thirst. At other times it only ever descends to move to a new tree or to take a quick mouthful of soil, swallowing the earth, or gravel, as an aid to digestion. It moves clumsily on the ground and is quick to return to the security of the branches.

So, for most of the time this remarkable animal must survive by getting all its moisture from the tough gum leaves on which it feeds. In fact its name "koala" refers to this. It comes from the old aboriginal habit of passing a water bowl round for everyone to take a drink. If one person in the group was not thirsty he would say "koala," meaning "no drink."

# The Whale

THE BIGGEST ANIMAL THAT HAS EVER LIVED ON THIS PLANET IS THE gigantic blue whale. It is even bigger than any of the monstrous dinosaurs that once roamed the earth many millions of years ago. Until you have seen one it is hard to imagine its size. The best way to understand it is to compare it with a more familiar animal, such as the elephant. One blue whale weighs as much as thirty-three fully grown elephants.

The record length for any whale is almost 109 feet, but there is a whole range of sizes, from the mighty blue, right down to the pygmy whale that is only about 8 feet long. There are over thirty species altogether, but the one we know best is the huge humpback whale that has allowed human swimmers to follow it closely and study its way of life. So what exactly is it like, this particular giant of the ocean?

Surprisingly, it is extremely docile and friendly. Stories from the early days of whaling told of savage monsters with a violent character. Modern scientists who were the first to try and get really near to swimming whales were no doubt afraid their boats would be crushed, but they soon found there was little to worry about. Of course, if the early whalers were firing harpoons into the animals and causing them great pain, it is very likely that some of them did turn and attack their tormentors. Left alone, we now know that these powerful creatures are quiet and shy.

The most amazing single fact about the humpback whale is that its brain is five times bigger than that of a human being. It is not clear why it needs such a large brain, although it may have something to do with the complicated way in which each whale keeps in touch with its companions and tells them about its changing moods.

Because whales have only flippers and fins, instead of arms and legs, it is difficult for us to guess from body language how they think. Our own moods are expressed through the gestures we make with our wonderfully precise fingers and thumbs, and through our changing facial expressions. The whale cannot make gestures or facial expressions. And the noises it produces are so strange that we cannot easily grasp their meaning. It may be extremely brainy, but how can it let us know about its feelings? We have yet to solve this problem.

The first sight we get of a swimming whale is often the tall spout of water that squirts up from its nose. Its nostril is called a blow-hole and, every time the whale breathes, the moist air from its lungs is shot up out of this hole at an astonishing speed of 300 miles an hour. In this way a big whale can empty its lungs and take in fresh air very quickly. An average-sized whale can take a deep breath that is three thousand times as big as a human breath and can do this in two seconds.

Being a warm-blooded mammal and not a fish means that all whales have to come to the surface to breathe from time to time. Many whales only dive for five to ten minutes, but some of the biggest have been known to stay down for over an hour and to reach great depths in the ocean.

No animal in the world has such great freedom of movement as the mighty whale, except for human beings. Most animals are restricted to small home ranges or are hemmed in by quarrelsome neighbors, but for the big whales the whole ocean is their home and they can wander fearlessly wherever they like – just so long as they do not come across a deadly whaling ship.

Individual whales are often easy to recognize because of the strange white markings on their heads and bodies. These marks are not part of the whale itself, but are small animals that have attached themselves to its skin, just as they do to the bottom of boats. They are barnacles that live and breed there permanently. The whale seems unable to remove them and must put up with them all through its long life. An old whale may have to carry as much as 1,000 pounds of these marine hitchhikers.

Despite its huge size, the humpback whale feeds entirely on tiny shrimps called krill. These little animals are non-stop swimmers that gather in vast swarms near the surface of the ocean. The swarms are sometimes over a mile long and contain countless millions of shrimps. After feeding on them, a big whale will have gathered several tons of krill in its stomach. It has a large filter inside its mouth which separates the mass of shrimps from the water.

If it is not feeling particularly energetic, the feeding whale can obtain a good meal simply by swimming along near the surface of the water with its gigantic mouth wide open, letting the shrimps drift quietly into its gaping jaws.

At other times, it may catch them in three special ways. The first is called lunge-feeding. The whale opens its mouth as wide as possible and then plunges straight into the mass of small creatures as they float in a dense cloud in the sea.

The second is called flick-feeding. When it switches to this method, it uses its enormous tail to flick the krill into its mouth.

The third is called bubble-netting and is hard to believe unless you have seen it with your own eyes. The whale swims down below the swarm of floating krill and then begins to move slowly up towards it, circling round and round as it does so. It swims in a spiral, so that the circles get smaller as it comes close to the surface of the water. All the time it is doing this, it is blowing out a stream of small bubbles, which rise up and form a circular 'net', trapping the krill inside the circle. Then, at the last moment, the whale opens its mouth wide and, with a final, powerful upward thrust, shoots straight up through the middle of the bubble-net. All the krill that have been squeezed together in the trap are easily swallowed in a single, massive gulp. The whale's great tongue is used to press them down into its throat.

The 40-ton whales feast like this for seven or eight months of the year. Sometimes they may continue feeding for as long as eighteen hours at a stretch. They do this in the colder, northern waters, where krill are plentiful.

Then, in the winter, they move south, swimming majestically for hundreds of miles until they come to their breeding grounds. One group of about four hundred of them move down to the Pacific Ocean each year until they reach the tropical islands

of Hawaii. They gather there in November, remaining in the warmer waters until the following March. Throughout this entire time the adult whales do not feed at all.

During this breeding season, they pass their days basking, playing, resting, courting and giving birth. The males spend many hours singing very loud songs, the sounds of which can be heard hundreds of miles away, across the ocean. The noises they make can be deep boomings and rumblings, or higher, more squeaky screeches. Sometimes they groan and sometimes they moo and twitter. The sound of a humpback whale in full song is like nothing else on earth.

They keep varying the sounds, rather like humans making music. A male will sometimes continue singing non-stop for over half an hour, as though it is composing a symphony. Each group of whales has its own local song-style, and these styles change slightly from year to year.

So extraordinary is this musical talent of the humpback whales that a recording of one of their songs has been placed on the spaceship Voyager, which has already flown out past Jupiter. It has been sent as a special message from this planet to anyone in outer space who might be able to hear it and appreciate it.

Because this remarkable whale-song is never heard during the long feeding season in northern waters, it clearly has some sort of courtship message, the males advertising their presence to females near and far. Although they may grunt and whistle at any time of the year, as a way of keeping in touch, the full song only appears when they are breeding.

The courtship of the humpback whale is an amazing spectacle. The gigantic animals can be seen leaping playfully from the water. Sometimes they make a great

din by beating the surface of the water with their flippers or their tails, or they may display by rolling their huge bodies from side to side.

From time to time, they pause to stroke one another's bodies and, once in a while, they slap their partners affectionately. These slaps, which can be heard miles away across the sea, are no more than tender caresses between the courting animals.

When it is born, the baby humpback whale measures about 16 feet from head to tail, and is ten times as long as a human baby. It is nursed by its mother for nearly a year, until it has reached a length of about 26 feet. She is a very loving mother, and has been seen to protect her baby from danger by wrapping her long flipper around its young body.

Once the breeding is over, the whales set off north for another long summer shrimp-feast, moving at a speed of about five miles an hour, and taking their new babies with them. The pregnant females are the first to go, followed by the young adults and the males. The mothers with their new babies are the last to leave, lingering just a little longer in the friendly warmth of the tropical waters before facing the icy cold of the feeding grounds.

There used to be 100,000 humpback whales in the world's oceans, but they were harpooned and slaughtered so savagely that their numbers sank lower and lower until there were only a few thousand left. Then, in 1966, a worldwide agreement was made to stop all hunting of these magnificent animals. Since then they have been able to live in peace and their numbers have improved slightly.

Today it is thought that there are altogether about 4,000 humpback whales alive. Some of these are so old that they carry scars where harpoons hit but failed to kill them, back in the bad old whaling days.

The whales' future is not as certain as it could be, because there are still some nations that would like to start hunting them again, but we now know so much more about these gentle, intelligent giants, that most of us have gained great respect for them. And it is this new respect that is their best hope for survival. Whoever tries to slaughter them now will have to face the anger of the rest of the world.

# The Lion

ALTHOUGH THE LION IS THE MOST FAMOUS MEMBER OF THE CAT FAMILY, IN its way of life it is not very cat-like. A typical cat is found in dense undergrowth, hunts alone and lives a solitary existence. A typical dog is found in more open country, hunts in a pack and lives a highly social life. In these respects, the lion is more dog-like than cat-like. It prefers open grasslands, hunts in a group and lives in a pride of between ten and thirty animals.

In a typical pride there are between five and ten adult females with their cubs, and several adult males. The females do most of the hunting. The males do most of the fighting. The cubs pass most of their waking hours playing.

When the food supply is plentiful it is an easy life, and the whole pride spends an enormous amount of time resting and sleeping. Lions sleep twice as long as humans do. We usually need about eight hours every night. A lion will slumber for a total of sixteen hours out of every twenty-four. Unlike us, most of this snoozing is done during the heat of the day.

As the sun sets, the pride stirs. In the half-light the lionesses leave their tiny cubs and set off in search of prey. They work as a team. As soon as they have spotted a herd of antelopes they fan out sideways and begin to creep slowly towards them. The sandy color of the hunters' bodies makes them almost invisible in the long, dry grasses of the African plains.

Their eyesight is very sharp and they watch intently as the herd feeds. If an antelope stops grazing and looks up in alarm, suspecting that danger is near, the lionesses all "freeze" in their tracks. They lower their bodies as far as possible. Crouching in the clumps of grass, they keep their eyes fixed firmly on the prey and remain completely still. The antelope sniffs the air, trying to detect the smell of a killer. If it fails to do so, it returns to feeding once more. At this, the lionesses all start creeping forward again.

As they advance, little by little, the lionesses move at different speeds. The ones in the middle of the group go forward slower. The ones on the extreme left and the extreme right move quicker. The result of this is that they start to encircle their prey. This is the method of hunting sometimes used by wolves.

When they are as close as they can get, they break cover and charge forward, leaping towards their victims at nearly 40 miles an hour. The antelopes panic and dash in all directions. Now each lioness works on her own, trying to catch up with a particular antelope, slap it to the ground with a mighty paw, and grab its neck in her powerful jaws.

Although at this stage the hunters do not take much notice of their companions, they are still a great help to one another. This is because the prey animals see the attacks coming from different directions at the same time and are thrown into confusion, not knowing which way to turn. This chaos helps the hunters.

If the herd of antelopes could flee in a more organized way, with all the animals racing away in the same direction at top speed, they could easily out-run the lions. Nearly all the big animals on which lions prey are faster than they are, sometimes as much as 10 miles an hour quicker. So a group attack has much the best chance of succeeding. Even so, lions are only successful in about one out of four hunts.

When the prey is caught it is held down by a bite to the throat that stops the animal breathing. Quietly, in a few moments, the antelope is dead. After a short pause, the pride starts feasting. The females share the meat between them. If one of the big males comes up to look at the kill, he will also eat his fill. With a large enough prey, such as a big antelope, a zebra or a buffalo, there is plenty of food for everyone. In no time at all the bellies of the lions are huge and rounded. Then they must rest again, digesting the fresh meat and cleaning the blood from their faces and paws. Soon slumber returns, until after a few hours the animals feel thirsty and leave together for a visit to the nearest water-hole.

Lions usually rest on the ground but sometimes, when it is very hot, they look for a higher place where they can perhaps enjoy a cooling breeze. Often they lie out on top of a rocky outcrop, or they may even climb up into the lower branches of a tree. This not only helps to keep them cool, it also gives them a good lookout position.

The males of the pride have to be on the alert for other, younger males prowling around searching for a group of females to call their own. If the younger males feel they can scare off the pride-owning males, they will threaten them and, if necessary, fight them for the right to take over the pride. The intruders will probably be driven away by the pride males, but from time to time there are changes. If the pride-owners are getting too old or have been injured, it may be possible for the newcomers to defeat them. It is during these fights that the great black manes of the males are so important. These not only protect the necks of the animals from savage blows, they also make the lions look bigger and more frightening to their enemies.

The hairy manes are ideal for this because they have the special advantage of increasing the size of the lions without making them much heavier. If the bodies of the males grew any bigger they would become too clumsy, but the long black hairs of the mane add hardly any extra weight, even though they give the impression of huge size.

If the new males win their struggle, the first act they perform as the new owners of the pride is to kill and eat all the young cubs. These cubs belong to the old males, now removed, and the new males are determined not to waste their energies rearing the cubs of other fathers.

As a result of this slaughter of the cubs, the females stop giving milk. As soon as this has happened, they are ready to mate again. They do this with the new males and, in just over a hundred days, these males themselves become the fathers of a new batch of cubs. This means that, after the new births, they will be looking after their own young and not those of other lions. If they did not remove the original cubs, the females would continue feeding them with their milk and this would stop them from mating. So the massacre speeds up the "take-over" by the new males.

The old males who are driven out of their family groups often end up living on their own. These solo lions are a pathetic sight. They are forced to feed on easy prey, animals that can be caught without any help from hunting companions. Sometimes they kill slow-moving creatures such as porcupines, only to find themselves with a nose full of quills. Captive lions in zoos may not have much space in which to wander, but they do at least have the chance to visit the zoo vet when they are in pain. In the wild, during his last days, the "lord of the jungle" must nearly always suffer pain and indignity.

The new males that have taken over a pride are as kind and caring about their own cubs as they are savage towards the cubs of others. They allow their offspring to play near them and even to bite their tails, without too much complaint.

Every night at sunset they patrol their territory, leaving their mark upon it. They do this by spraying urine on trees, logs, rocks and other suitable landmarks. They also announce their presence by loud roaring. This bellowing warns off the other lions living nearby. It goes on for about an hour at dusk and can be heard again at dawn.

Other sounds made by lions include a soft grunting call given when the members of the group wish to keep in touch with one another. If their companions are hidden, either by the undergrowth during the day, or by the darkness at night, these little grunts act as a signal saying simply "I am over here."

In more intimate moments, lions can be heard to utter their version of a domestic cat's purr, which sounds like a tender rumbling noise. If they are irritated they growl and snarl. If they are about to attack one another they make a sharp coughing sound that spells serious trouble. And if a mother is calling out to her cubs, she uses a little moaning noise, saying "where are you," "come here" or "keep up with me."

Lions are the easiest of all the cats to breed in captivity and zoos often have more of them than they know what to do with. They are also still common enough in tropical Africa, but in other parts of the world they have almost vanished.

The last lions in Britain were killed off by Stone Age human hunters some fifty thousand years ago. They disappeared from most of the rest of Europe not long after this, although they did manage to survive in Greece until little more than two thousand years ago. The North African, or Barbary lion was reduced to small numbers by the Romans, who used them for sport and for killing prisoners in the arena. The last surviving lions in North Africa were destroyed within the last hundred years.

There may still be a few stragglers left in the most remote regions of the Middle East, but this is unlikely. The last lion seen in that part of the world was sighted in 1941 in Iran.

The only wild lions that are definitely known to exist outside tropical Africa today are in one small region of western India, the Gir Forest. Once there were huge numbers of lions all across Asia, but by 1900 every one of them had been killed except a group of about a hundred in this special reserve. These were carefully protected and when counted recently numbered 162. It is hoped to move some of them to sanctuaries at other locations in India, to ensure that the Asian lion survives long into the future, even if, with its tiny numbers, it is only a sad reminder of its former glory.

# The Bison

THE BISON IS THE LARGEST OF ALL THE LAND ANIMALS OF NORTH AMERICA. A big male can weigh over 2,000 pounds. Before the coming of the white man, the great plains of North America were swarming with them. The huge herds could stretch for over 50 miles, and were often so tightly packed that they made the grasslands look black.

The massive head of the bison is held low on its heavily-built shoulders. There is a pair of short, curved horns, with the tips pointing inwards. Beneath the jaws there is a shaggy beard and on the humped shoulders the fur is long and thick, almost like a lion's mane.

The "mane" reaches down around the front legs, which look as though they are wearing hairy trousers. By contrast, the rear end of the animal has much shorter hair. This special arrangement of the bison's coat means that it can keep warm by turning into the wind.

Every year the vast herds of literally millions of these animals moved north in the summer and then, when the weather began to get cold, south again for winter grazing. On each trip they traveled several hundred miles.

Each summer they mated and each spring the cows produced their reddish-colored calves. At birth, the calves lacked the great fleshy humps of the adults. These humps did not start to grow until the young animals were about three months old. Weaned from their mothers' milk after one year, the young adults would themselves begin breeding at two to three years of age and, without accidents or attacks by wolves, could hope to live for about thirty years.

In those early days, the worst enemies of the herds were the flies and ticks that infested their thick fur. The bison did their best to defeat these pests by creating huge wallows in which they could roll and coat themselves with healing mud. When it was too dry for mud, they used dust-wallows instead. They also rubbed themselves against trees or rocks to relieve their skin irritations. Sometimes, when the pests were very troublesome, the heavy-bodied bison did this so vigorously that they seriously damaged or even destroyed the trees they used.

When mankind arrived on the scene, in the shape of the first American Indians, the bison herds faced a new enemy. Being a grass-eating member of the cattle family, the bison's meat was excellent to eat. Many of the Indians settled on the American plains and became bison-hunters.

Their whole way of life became controlled by the herds. As well as eating the bison meat, they covered their homes in bison skins, they wore bison clothing, slept under bison coverings, sat on bison rugs and crossed rivers in bison-skin boats. The animals also gave them the string for their bows, glue, thread, rope, water-vessels and saddles.

Despite the fact that they had to kill many bison with their traps and their bows and arrows, there were too few of these Indians to cause any serious damage to the herds. The animals could breed fast enough to cover their losses. There was still a natural balance. But all this was to change with the coming of their next enemy – the white man.

Before the European settlers appeared, there had been between 60 and 100 million bison in North America. After the arrival of guns, the number soon dropped to 40 million. But this was only the beginning. A mass slaughter was about to take place. It is hard to believe, but within twenty years the teeming millions of bison were to be reduced to only a few hundred animals. Some give the figure as 541, others as 835. A whole species had been practically wiped from the face of the earth. It was the greatest destruction of wildlife ever known.

Why did it happen? There was more than one reason. When we see a Wild West movie, with cowboys and Indians fighting one another, we imagine that this is how the newcomers "won the West," but it was not. The way the West was conquered was quite simply by setting out to destroy the bison herds.

The first thing that the new settlers from Europe noticed when they started moving into the homelands of the Indians was how much the inhabitants depended on the bison. They saw how their whole society was based on products taken from these animals. So, all that the new arrivals had to do was to shoot the bison and the Indians would be defeated. That is what happened, and it took place at lightning speed.

Even where the Indians were not a problem, there were other reasons for killing the bison: for meat, for clothes, or simply for sport. The new farmers had an extra reason, for they had brought with them their domestic cattle and these newly imported grass-eaters needed the plains on which to feed. So, for this reason too the bison had to go.

Also, the railroads that were being built, from the east to the west, crossed right through bison lands. Laying these tracks, over huge distances through wild country, was a major problem. Thousands of men were involved, slaving away in the heat. The labor was hard and the men needed good meals if they were to work well. So the railroad companies brought in special hunters who were expert at killing the nearby bison to provide food for their work-force.

The most famous bison-hunter was a man known as Buffalo Bill. ("Buffalo" was the local name given to the bison.) His real name was William Cody and he wrote of his work: "I killed buffalo for the railroad company for twelve months and during that time . . . I had killed 4,280 buffalo." Of course there were many such hunters. Between them they killed more than a million bison a year, until there was only a handful of sad stragglers left alive. The day of the bison was over.

Luckily, these last few survivors were saved before it was too late. They were protected and used as the starting point of a major rescue operation. By the early part of this century they had bred so well that their numbers were back up into the thousands again. Today there are about 30,000 bison in special game reserves and

parks, where visitors can go to see them and try to imagine what 100 million must once have looked like, spread out over the prairies of North America.

We nearly destroyed the bison for good, but for once there is a happy ending and these magnificent animals are now safe for the future.

# The Giraffe

ANYONE WHO HAS SEEN A BABY GIRAFFE ENTER THE WORLD WILL NEVER forget the moment. It is one of the most extraordinary births in the animal world. The mother does nothing to help. She seems to take little notice of what is happening. Instead of making the arrival easier by lying down, she remains standing, staring into the distance. Her first concern is to check the horizon for possible dangers.

Everything has to happen quickly, before any killers arrive on the scene. The baby is born in a rush, its body crashing to the ground below in a tangle of legs and hooves. Its shape makes its birth difficult. Inside its mother, just before it is born, its long neck is pressed tight against its equally long front legs. As the birth begins, the feet appear first, then the head follows. After a brief pause the rest of the lanky body slips out and its weight – as much as twenty human babies – pulls it clear.

It hits the ground with such force, that it seems certain it must be hurt. Happily this never happens. Within a few moments, the calf is blinking at the strange new world around it. It lies still for several minutes, breathing the outside air for the first time. Then, rather shakily, it starts trying to struggle to its feet. It may manage this in as little as five minutes. Some calves take longer, perhaps as much as half an hour.

As soon as the new baby has heaved itself up and is standing – 6.5 feet tall – on its spindly legs, it begins to totter forward. It moves shakily about, this way and that, looking rather like an acrobat learning to walk on stilts. Very quickly it manages to control itself and takes its first, faltering steps towards its mother. She watches it closely now, and leans down to lick its still wet body with her long tongue. She sniffs it, too, getting to know its special smell.

In no time at all, the baby giraffe is contentedly feeding from its mother. In a matter of hours it will be able to run and play and walk alongside her. The most dangerous phase of its life is now over.

Growth is rapid for the prancing young giraffe and by the time it is a year old it will have doubled its height. Within three years it will have reached almost adult height. It can then hope to live for about twenty-five years, if it does not suffer from some unusual accident.

The adult giraffe is the tallest animal in the world today. The record is held by a big male called George whose head almost touched the roof of his zoo home, which was 21.5 feet high. So, if three men stood on one another's shoulders, the top one would still have to look up to see George's face.

Most giraffes do not grow quite so big, but they are still amazingly tall compared with any other animal. The average height for a bull giraffe is about 16.5 feet. Cow giraffes are slightly smaller – only about 14 feet.

The advantage of being so tall is that the animals can reach high up into the trees when they are browsing on leaves and shoots. Lower down, among the bushes, many different kinds of plant-eating animals can nibble the greenery and must compete with one another for food, but for the lofty giraffes there are no rivals. They can munch away contentedly in a skyscraper world of their own.

Male and female giraffes feed in a different way from one another. The males stretch their necks up as high as possible, while the females lean forward at an angle. This means that the two sexes can feed at slightly different levels, the females below the males. Because of this, they can remain close when browsing without getting in one another's way.

Using this method, the animals can spend hours stripping off and swallowing leaf after leaf without any interference. Wherever there are green, leafy trees, these long-necked giants are able to enjoy a daily feast – and there is always more than they can ever want to eat.

This is just as well because they need a great deal of food and spend about twelve

out of every twenty-four hours eating. On a good day they will each consume about 140 pounds of vegetation – a huge amount – ripping it off with their long black tongues.

These tongues are powerful and sticky with saliva, and the giraffes can stretch them for a full 18 inches out of their mouths when they are searching for food. They can be curled around individual leaves and shoots and can quickly tug them loose. Even the sharpest thorns and spikes cannot stop them.

Most of their feeding is done by day, but on moonlit evenings, they can be seen gently browsing the night away, moving like great slender ghosts through the trees.

Many people have wondered how giraffes sleep. Do they lie down like other hoofed animals, or do they sleep standing up? And how do they rest their long necks? The answer is that they can doze either standing or lying down, and this dozing is a sort of half-sleep. But it is not complete, deep sleep. For this they lie down and twist their necks back and around, rather like slumbering birds. Their heads come to rest on their rumps and they stay like this for about five minutes at a time. They cannot afford to sleep for very long because of the danger of night-prowling killers. Short naps are all they can risk, and they usually only manage a total of about half an hour of deep sleep each night. For a giraffe, however, this is quite enough, when combined with the much longer periods spent dozing and half-sleeping.

Giraffes in the wild enjoy the luxury of having a small alarm-clock in the shape

of the tiny oxpecker or tick bird. This lives on their backs, where it carries out the important task of pecking at and removing any small parasites it can find. It also raises the alarm with its noisy crying, when it sees danger approaching. This quickly wakens the slumbering giraffe, which can then leap up and escape before the killer draws too close.

During the daytime, when it is fully awake, an adult giraffe has few enemies to fear. Even the mighty lion thinks twice about attacking one. With a single kick of its huge feet, a bull giraffe is quite capable of killing even the strongest lion, and the big cats nearly always keep a respectful distance. Only the baby giraffes are easy targets for the prowling hunters, and about half of the young ones are killed before they reach the age of six months. Many more would die, were it not for the protection of their ever-alert mothers.

Giraffes have wonderful eyes, with color vision, and can see smaller animals clearly in the distance, even when they are over half a mile away. Combined with their long necks, their big eyes make it easy for them to keep a sharp lookout for any approaching danger.

Although they react violently to attacks from lions and other hunting animals, there is very little serious fighting between the giraffes themselves. The males may often engage in mock battles, swinging their necks at one another, but they seldom make contact. Only on very rare occasions, when a strange male has arrived from some faraway region, is there a real battle. Then the heads are used like massive clubs and deliver powerful sideways blows. The animals' skulls are strongly built to withstand these blows.

On top of the giraffe's head are short, blunt, hair-covered horns and these can be used to hammer an opponent. In the old Giraffe House at the London Zoo there used to be a deep dent in the wooden panelling on the wall, caused by a blow delivered at a keeper many years ago. It seems that, for a zoo giraffe, its human companion is sometimes looked upon as a possible rival and once in a while the animal wants to remind him who is the boss. Luckily, because of the great length of its neck, its aim does not appear to be too accurate when attacking humans.

Some people imagine that the giraffe has a large number of bones in its neck, but this is not true. In fact, it has no more than any other hoofed animal. As with all its short-necked relatives, there are only seven neck-bones, but each of these is, of course, much longer than the similar bones in a deer or an antelope.

The giraffe's long neck, so useful for feeding, creates something of a problem when it comes to drinking. Living in the hot grasslands and broken woodlands of tropical Africa, the animals need to drink at a water-hole every day. They may have to trek for several miles to get there, but the journey is a vital part of their daily routine.

Once they have arrived at the water's edge, the giraffes must adopt a clumsy posture with their front legs spread wide apart, as if they are about to do the splits. Feeling helpless in this position they are rather nervous and keep bringing their heads up to look around for possible enemies.

Raising their heads quickly from the water level could easily make them faint, were it not for the fact that they have very special blood vessels in their necks. These vessels can close themselves down to prevent the blood rushing away from their heads.

Once the giraffes return to the cover of the trees, they feel much safer. The color patterns of their coats, when seen in the half-light of dusk or dawn, help them blend in with the background. These patterns may look vivid to us when we see a giraffe close-up in a zoo in bright daylight, but in the dim evening or early morning light, they do help to hide the huge animals from the eyes of killers prowling in the distance.

If, despite their coat colors, the hunting animals start to approach too closely, the giraffes still have their long legs to save them. At full gallop, adults can reach speeds of up to 40 miles an hour and can outrun most enemies with ease.

During the bright light of the African day, the patterns on the animals' coats help them in a completely different way. Then they act as labels. If you look closely at the net-like design of the giraffe's markings, with the pale lines surrounding small patches of reddish-brown color, you will soon see that each giraffe has a special pattern all of its own. It is very likely that one giraffe can identify another by these "personal" patterns, just as humans can be identified by their unique fingerprints. The pattern of each individual giraffe never alters from its birth until its death.

One of the strangest features of the giraffe is that it is almost completely silent. Being such a huge animal, one would expect it to roar or bellow, but the best it can manage is an occasional grunt, gurgle, whistle, hiss or snort. Baby giraffes in distress can produce a little bleating sound and that is about as noisy as this extraordinary animal ever gets.

The first giraffe ever to be seen in Europe was brought back from Africa by Julius Caesar after he had installed Cleopatra on the throne of Egypt. The Roman crowds were astonished by the sight of the amazing animal as it was paraded through the crowded streets of the great city. They had never seen anything like it before, and were puzzled by its strange shape and markings. One famous Roman poet declared that it must be a cross between a camel and a leopard and it became known as the "camelopard," a name which lasted for centuries. Eventually, when it was realized how mistaken this idea was, "camelopard" was replaced by the Arab name of "giraffe" and we have kept that ever since.

# The Wolf

A THOUSAND YEARS AGO WOLVES ROAMED THE BRITISH COUNTRYSIDE. The bodies on the ground after the Battle of Hastings were said to have been devoured by the wolves from the nearby forests. Even Londoners felt unsafe and certain people living just outside the great city were given free land in exchange for destroying the local wolf-packs.

In an early *Book of Beasts*, written about eight hundred years ago, the wolf is described as a savage, blood-thirsty monster, always ready to attack and devour any human being it meets. "They massacre anybody who passes by with a fury of greediness," says the author and no doubt his frightened readers believed every word.

Back in those days, January was called "Wolf Month" because it was said to be the time when the wolves were most dangerous. It was also the start of the wolf-hunting season. Up and down the country, the hunters and trappers were out in the woods and forests, busily killing as many wolves as they could.

The tormented animals were driven back and back until they could only hold on in the very far north of Scotland and in some of the more remote areas of Ireland. Then, about two hundred years ago, even those tough survivors were tracked down and destroyed. The wild wolf was gone forever from the British countryside.

In other parts of the world, it has also been under attack from men armed with better and better weapons. Today its only remaining stronghold is in the harsh lands of the north. Even there, in the freezing forests and the ice-cold wastelands, it is becoming less common. One day, it will probably vanish altogether, because human beings seem to fear and hate it so much.

Why do we feel like this towards the wolf? Is it really such a monster? To find the answer it helps to look back at the way our own feeding habits have changed.

Once humans were all hunters, like the wolves. Then about 10,000 years ago farming was invented. This was much more convenient than hunting because animals were kept in pens and fields, and could be killed and eaten whenever needed. There was now hardly any need to hunt wild animals as food.

This was fine for the farmers, and unfortunately it was also fine for the nearby wolves. The domestic animals, neatly penned in, were easy prey for them too. Over and over again, the livestock was attacked by hungry wolves, especially in winter. The wolf became the greatest enemy of these new farmers and they fought back as hard as they could. They also started to invent wild stories about man-eating wolves, turning the animal into a terrifying villain. This helped to whip up more and more wolf-hatred and to keep the war against it going at full blast.

Even today, we still have the leftovers of that war with us. Many people continue to think of the wolf as a savage enemy, with a lust for human blood. As small children we are frightened by the story of Red Riding Hood and, when we are a little older, we gasp at the horrors of the werewolves we watch at the cinema.

How do these old legends and tall tales compare with the real thing? What is the wolf really like?

Perhaps the most startling fact about wolves is that it is almost impossible to find a genuine case of any person being killed by one. It is very likely that wolves did eat some of the bodies left lying on old battlefields, but they do not do the killing themselves. Humans are not suitable prey for wolves and are left strictly alone.

In reality, the character of the wolf is not "savage" but "timid." Wolves are incredibly cautious creatures that will slink away from men if given half a chance. Even a tame wolf, that has been reared from a tiny cub by a devoted human owner, will be nervous with strangers. An ordinary pet dog is far more bold.

If it is a shy, retiring creature, how can we find out about its way of life? In the last few years, a number of rugged and long-suffering scientists have visited the freezing Arctic wilds, where packs of wolves still roam, and have spent many long weeks and months quietly watching, filming, photographing and making notes about everything the animals do. They have now been able to give us, at last, a true picture of the way of life of the wild wolf.

Wolf cubs are born in the early spring. They are blind and helpless and need a great deal of loving care and protection.

Three weeks before their mother is about to give birth she starts digging frantically in the earth, preparing a special den for the cubs deep underground. Choosing a place where there is a strong roof for the new den – in the shape of a tree-trunk, some tree-roots, or a big rock – she first makes an entrance 3 feet long. This gets narrower as it goes deeper. Then she makes a long, slender tunnel that runs for about 9 feet before it broadens out into the nest-chamber. In this round cavity, safe and snug, she gives birth to her litter of four to seven tiny cubs.

If she has the chance, the she-wolf prefers to make her den on sloping ground above a river, or some other source of water. She will need to drink a great deal when she is nursing her cubs. If possible she will make the tunnel in her den rise upwards towards the cavity where she will be giving birth. In this way flooding can be avoided. No matter how hard it rains outside, the water will not flow into the nest-chamber. Her cubs will be safe while the storms rage outside.

If the mother is disturbed in her den, even in the slightest way, she takes emergency action. She picks up one of the cubs in her mouth and carries it away to a second den that she has prepared earlier. She returns and moves the second cub, then the third, and so on, until all have been taken to safety. After moving all her cubs, she always pays one last visit to the old den, making doubly sure that it really is empty.

This two-den system is a special insurance against enemies discovering the original home and raiding it. The cubs themselves help in their own protection after they have passed a few weeks in their "secret bunker." They do this by digging a whole network of small tunnels that provide extra escape routes and cross-connections. We know that these tunnels are built by the cubs and not by their mother because the passages are too narrow to allow an adult wolf to squeeze along them.

After three or four weeks the young cubs have grown a great deal and emerge cautiously from the entrance-cave of their burrow. Peering around at the outside world, they stagger about on unsteady legs. They are now ready to begin exploring this fascinating new scene that lies stretched out in front of them.

Quickly, all the other members of the pack come crowding round to meet the newcomers. Their greetings are always friendly, but sometimes they can become a little too friendly. Both the mother and the father of the cubs will keep a close eye on what is happening and prevent any interference that might become too exhausting for their offspring.

As the cubs grow up, various members of the wolf-pack will bring food offerings for them. Others will groom them and clean them, and still others will play with them. Already the cubs are being taken into the social life of the group and made to feel at home there. By the time they are five months old they are allowed to travel with the pack.

Being helpful to one another is one of the special features of wolf society, and it is not only the young cubs that are given assistance. When the she-wolf is forced to stay in her den giving birth, the other adults in the pack will bring her food after they have been hunting.

The hunt itself is the most important part of a wolf's life. During the summer months, many wolves can chase and catch small animals by themselves, without the help of their companions. But during the colder months, when all the small prey animals are hidden underground, hunger drives the wolves to track down bigger prey, such as deer. A wolf cannot kill a large deer single-handed. It is forced to hunt in a group if it is to be successful.

This group-hunting starts with a pack of wolves moving off together, searching for their prey. On a difficult hunt they may travel for over 20 miles. Eventually the leader smells a distant deer. The animal can be detected by odor alone when it is $1\frac{1}{2}$ miles away, if the wolves are approaching into the wind. The leader stops in his tracks and remains very still.

What happens next is very strange. All the wolves pause and, like their leader, point their heads in the direction of the faraway prey. Their noses sniff the air, their eyes stare and their ears are pricked forward. Then they perform a special ritual. They all cluster together like football players in a huddle. Standing nose-to-nose they wait for a few seconds with their tails wagging excitedly. What passes between them at this moment we do not know, but soon they break away and set off directly towards the scent of the prey animal.

As the pack nears the prey they become highly excited but they manage to control themselves. They do nothing rash. They keep staring forward, wagging their tails and trying not to alert the deer. They must get as close as they possibly can before the prey realizes they are there.

If the prey sees them and tries to flee they will be after it in a bounding dash of speed. If it holds its ground, they are much more wary and usually just stand and watch the animal. It is the act of fleeing that triggers their attack.

They try to bring the animal down as quickly as possible, but if it is an athletic runner they may have to keep after it for a long time. If, during this high-speed part of the hunt, they fail to catch up with the prey in about half a mile, they nearly always give up, but some packs have been known to keep the chase going for as far as 5 miles.

One of the secrets of their success as hunters is that they can run and run without tiring. If they have to, they simply wear their prey out. Despite this ability, they much prefer a short chase and a quick kill and this is what nearly always happens.

In the kill itself, the wolves overtake the running prey and lunge at its body, biting at its sides, rump, shoulders and nose. When they pull it down they tear it to pieces and feast on the meat. Each wolf gobbles down all it can manage – sometimes as much as 20 pounds of flesh – and its belly becomes swollen and heavy. What the pack cannot eat they may bury in the earth or snow. Then they can return later, dig it up and finish their meal.

Living such a cooperative social life, the wolf has to have a good "language" of signs and signals. Each animal must be able to tell its companions about its changing moods. This is done by a whole series of different actions, expressions and postures, most of which are very similar to those you can see in any pet dog. Modern dogs are, after all, little more than domesticated wolves.

Because wolves have such powerful jaws and teeth, as part of their prey-hunting weaponry, they have to avoid fights among themselves wherever possible. If they did not do this, they could easily wound or kill one another. Submissive gestures are therefore extremely important. These are postures and expressions that say "I give in, do not hurt me, you are the boss." A weak animal can say this by crouching low, pulling back its mouth corners, lowering its ears and tucking its tail between its legs.

If it wants to be even more submissive, it can flatten its body on the ground. Going even further it can turn itself upside-down and look up at its opponent. Few top wolves will attack a companion that displays itself in this way. The submissive action allows a disagreement to be settled without bloodshed. Both wolves live to hunt another day. The weaker one may have lost face, and will have to give way to the other animal at all times, but at least it is alive and is not lame or wounded.

A dominant animal does the opposite of a weak one. It stands tall, bristles its fur, making itself look even bigger, and snarls. It pulls its upper lip up, exposing its huge fangs. Its ears are pricked and its tail is raised stiffly in the air.

These are just some of the many signs that wolves make to one another as they sort out their squabbles. The result is a pack in which each animal knows its own place, is bossy to some and bossed by others. This way of sorting out their relations makes it easier for them to cooperate when they are setting off on the hunt.

The pack also has special signals that tell other packs to keep off their home territory. This is mostly done by scent-marking, the territory-owners cocking their

legs and squirting scented urine on to landmarks such as trees and bushes.

They also advertise their presence by group howling. One member of the pack tosses its head back and lets out an ear-piercing howl. Quickly the others join it until together they are creating a din so loud that it can be heard as far as 6 miles away. Since most wolf territories are about 6 miles across, this means that they can, in an instant, let all their neighbors know where they are and, in this way, avoid violent encounters with rival packs.

Clearly, the wolf is not the savage, uncontrolled monster of legend. Now that we understand it so much better, we can fear it less and respect it more. It is the ancient ancestor of all our four hundred breeds of modern dogs and this alone says something about its true nature. If it has given us "man's best friend" then it cannot be the villain it was once supposed to be. When it uses its sharp teeth it is only because it is hungry and hardly ever because it is angry. It is a model parent, a good companion, and a shy stranger. In the past it may have been the farmer's enemy, but today it should be looked upon instead as one of the most fascinating large animals that still survive in the wild, and given a chance to live out its life wherever there is a little wilderness to spare.

# The Hippo

HIPPOS ARE THE BIGGEST ANIMALS IN THE WORLD THAT LIVE IN FRESH WATER. They are found in the rivers and lakes of tropical Africa. An adult male hippo weighs up to 6,500 pounds. The female is slightly smaller.

Despite its huge size, the hippo does not eat a vast amount of food. This is because it lives such a lazy existence and hardly ever exerts itself. All day long it lies in the warm water, floating, basking on mud-flats, or gently swimming under the surface. The water supports its fat, sausage-shaped body and allows it to wallow the hours away without any effort. For much of the time its most energetic activity is yawning.

At night it leaves the water and plods slowly on to the grassy banks of the river where it spends five or six hours grazing on the succulent grasses. It always waits until well after sunset before making this move and is back in the safety of the water again long before sunrise. Usually all the hippos in a group have returned by 4:00 a.m. A few hungry ones may stay on for a little longer, but even they re-trace their steps before the first rays of light appear over the horizon.

It is the younger animals that spend most time on land, and the old, dominant males that are last out of the river and first back. Their role as defenders of the group territory seems to keep them in the water a little longer than the rest.

When on land, the hippo treads carefully along heavily-worn tracks that it knows well and which its short, tree-trunk legs have smoothed and flattened. Some of these pathways have been used by hippos for many years, the younger animals literally following in the footsteps of their ancestors. Along the sides of these paths are special piles of dung, where the adult hippos leave their personal scents as landmarks advertising their presence.

Each hippo travels several miles each night – sometimes as many as 15 miles if the search for food demands it. After it has plucked and swallowed its fill of grass stems, using its 20-inch-wide lips, and gobbled up any fallen fruit it may have been lucky enough to find, it then plods its way back down the same, familiar pathways and into the water to face another busy day's snoozing.

It sounds like a quiet, easy life for the hippo, but there are rare moments when it can suddenly become violent and noisy. This is when two male hippos disagree over who owns a particular patch of river.

Each male has a fixed territory which he controls. He lives there with his females and their young. Other males are not allowed to enter his area. If they do, they are immediately challenged and a terrible battle begins. It may last for well over an hour before one male – usually the owner of the patch – has managed to frighten off the intruder.

Hippo fights start out with bluff and counter-bluff. Angry males do not set about one another straight away. There is more show than actual contact. Before they begin charging and biting, they perform a whole series of special displays. Usually they can settle who is boss with these displays alone, but if two males are very equally matched, then, once in a while, there will be a serious bout of bloodthirsty sparring.

The most popular form of display is dunging. When two males meet at the border between their two kingdoms, they turn their rumps towards one another and then scatter their dung on the ground. The shape of the hippo's tail helps them to do this in a spectacular way, because it is flattened like a rudder. As they produce the dung, the short, stubby tail is flicked quickly from side to side. This spreads the hippo's droppings as far as possible. It may seem an odd way to threaten an enemy, but these droppings carry the personal odour of the displaying males and in this way they can tell one another about their condition and their aggressive state of mind.

If one of the males dares to advance on to a rival's stretch of river, then matters become more serious. Now the displays are dramatic, with furious forward charges and spectacular plunges through the water. Loud gruntings can be heard and the males start to rear up in the water and splash down again. They may blow water noisily out through their nostrils and toss huge mouthfuls of water up into the air.

Eventually, if neither will give way and retreat, they begin mouth-fighting, striking with their fearsome teeth at one another's faces and bodies. Many cuts and slashes can be made at this point and the naked skin starts to ooze blood. Fortunately the hippo's skin has good healing abilities and these wounds soon mend after the fighting is over.

At last, one male admits defeat and shows a humble lowering of the head and body. After he retreats, peace returns once more to the river and the lazy slumbering lifestyle of the hippos takes over again.

Hippos can sometimes be quite dangerous to humans as well as to rivals of their own kind. Small boats may be attacked and sunk if they are moving into the territory of a particularly aggressive male.

African tribesmen living near the great tropical rivers that are the hippos' homes, have for centuries hunted these huge animals for their meat. They have used both harpoons and spears to kill them and have often risked their lives in the process. The power of the animal's huge jaws is tremendous. An outraged hippo has been known to slice a man's body clean in two with a single bite.

When excited, hippos can swim with surprising speed, using dog-paddle actions of their heavy legs. Their clumsiness on land is replaced with surprising grace when they are advancing below the surface. Underwater film has shown us just how elegant the swimming hippo can be.

Their bodies are well designed for water-living. If you look at the animal's head you will notice that all the important sense organs are placed right on top of the skull. The short ears, the closeable nostrils and the big eyes can all be brought above the surface without any of the rest of the animal's body being visible from the river-bank. When they submerge completely they can easily stay down for five minutes and some people believe that, if necessary, they can remain below the water surface for up to fifteen minutes. Some even claim that they can manage half an hour below, but this may be an exaggeration.

The one weakness they have as aquatic animals is that they cannot deal with fast currents and must stay in slow-moving water. If they venture into the rapids they can easily be swept away and hurled down river, away from their special home territories.

In rare cases hippos have been swept out to sea and have then shown how, when forced out of their lazy lifestyle, they can swim strongly for very long distances. They have been known to travel from the coast of Africa to the island of Zanzibar, which is 22 miles away.

Sometimes, during the daytime, hippos like to haul themselves out of the water on to soft mud-banks and lie there like giant sun-bathers. When they do this they sometimes change color in a startling way. The smooth skin of the hippo is covered with special glands that produce a red liquid. This gave rise to an old saying that the hippo "sweats blood," but this is not true. The red pigment in the liquid is a special protection against sunburn – as though the animal has its own, built-in suntan oil. And this same liquid may also help to prevent infection in the many small wounds that appear after fighting.

The male hippo is called a bull, the female a cow and the baby a calf. Calves are usually born under water, and their first action after they emerge from the mother's body is to swim quickly to the surface and take a large gulp of air. Later, after they have recovered from the shock of being born, they start nuzzling the mother to find one of her two nipples. During their early days they are suckled under the water, where they are safe from any prowling killers.

The mother leaves her group and goes off to be on her own when she is due to give birth. After several weeks, she brings her infant back with her to the group, where it can play with the other youngsters. As it grows, the baby is allowed to perch on her back in the water, using her fat body like a huge stepping-stone as it views the world around it.

Many babies are killed before they are one year old. Their mothers do their best to defend them, but they do not always succeed. Their worst enemies are lions, leopards and hyenas. In rare cases crocodiles may attack them, but this is far less common than people used to think. If it is lucky enough to escape these killers and grow to full adult size, the hippo should be able to live a long life of up to fifty years.

There are two kinds of hippo alive today. In addition to the big one that lives all over tropical Africa, there is a rare pygmy hippo that is found only in a small area of West Africa. It is so tiny that twelve pygmy hippos would be needed to balance the weight of one ordinary hippo.

The pygmy hippo does not live in groups, like its large relative. Usually it is alone, but in the breeding season the male and female do spend some time together as a pair. Then the male leaves and the female brings up her calf by herself. As with the big hippo there is only a single baby.

Pygmy hippos are found in rivers deep inside dense, swampy forests and the tracks they make in the river-banks become so deep that they are almost like tunnels leading from the water to the feeding grounds. They are very shy and have seldom been seen in the wild.

The popular name "hippo" is short for "hippopotamus" which literally means "horse of the river." This was the name given to it by the ancient Greeks, who thought it was related to the horse. But they were wrong, because its nearest true relatives are the wild pigs. Despite this the old name has stayed with us, perhaps because the name "river pig" does not do justice to such a dramatic animal.

# The Cheetah

ONCE, MANY YEARS AGO, THERE WAS AN ARGUMENT AS TO WHICH COULD run faster, the greyhound or the cheetah. The greyhound is the fastest dog and the cheetah is the fastest cat, but which would be the winner if they were raced against one another? It is not easy to find the answer, because the greyhound is a domestic dog, used to racing around tracks, while the cheetah is a wild animal, used to the grasslands of tropical Africa.

Incredibly, it was possible to find a few cheetahs that were tame enough to run on a city racetrack. They were brought to London in 1937 and all was set for the great contest. The dog-owners were confident of victory, especially when they saw how the cheetahs disliked the tight bends on the oval-shaped track. They looked at their stop-watches and were pleased to see that their best greyhound had averaged nearly 37 miles an hour. But then, when they timed the best of the cheetahs, they were amazed to find that it was much faster and had clocked up just over 43 miles per hour. So, the best cat beat the best dog.

If the contest had been run on the open plains, the difference would have been even greater, because there cheetahs have been known to reach astounding speeds of between 50 and 60 miles an hour. In fact, there is nothing alive on four legs today that can match the cheetah. It is the champion sprinter of the entire animal world.

There is a special reason for this. Other members of the cat family, from the mighty tigers right down to tabby cats, all prefer to stalk their prey, hiding from them until the very last moment. Then they make a lightning dash over as short a distance as possible. The cheetah has to use a different way of hunting. It lives on the open plains where hiding is much more difficult. It may lie quietly in wait for prey at the beginning of a hunt, its spotted coat helping it to blend in with its background, but it can rarely get very close. Once it has broken cover it has to face a long sprint before it can hope to catch up with its victim. The average cheetah run is about 220 yards.

Its shape is well designed for this athletic lifestyle. It has a skinny, slender body, very long legs, and a lengthy tail that is used as a balancing aid. Its head is small and its ears are short and rounded. It is the only member of the cat family that is unable to sheath its claws. Like those of a dog, they are blunt and always visible. When the animal is running they help to give it a stronger grip on the earth.

When the cheetah is successful and manages to catch up with its prey — usually a fleet-footed antelope or gazelle — it knocks it to the ground with a swipe of one of its front legs. The prey is traveling so fast when this happens that it is thrown violently to the ground by the force of the blow. The cheetah then skids to a halt and pounces on it, grabbing its throat in its jaws.

At this point, the hunter pauses and stays still, keeping a firm grip on the prey's neck. This stops the victim from breathing and it quickly suffocates and dies. From the start of the chase to the final moment of death, it is all over in a matter of seconds.

If the successful hunter happens to be a female cheetah with half-grown cubs, she will allow them to share her kill. This means that she cannot always eat it at the spot where she brings it down. If possible, she will drag the body to a nearby bush, so that the family can feed there in peace, out of the hot sun and away from the eyes of other killers.

Smaller cubs are not allowed to follow their mother when she is hunting. They must stay hidden in a clump of long grass, or in a patch of undergrowth, when she sets off in search of food. There they must keep out of sight and wait quietly for her return. Every few days she moves them to a new hiding place, carrying them, one by one, firmly but gently in her jaws. Cheetahs are one-parent families, with the mother carrying out all the duties entirely on her own.

When they are very young, the cubs are delicate creatures with beautiful silver manes of hair that run right down the middle of their backs. There are usually three of them in a litter. At birth they can sheath their claws like any other member of the cat family. They only lose this ability when they are about ten weeks old. At about the same time their silver manes start to disappear and they soon look like miniature versions of their mother. They are weaned from the mother's milk at about three months. When they are two years old they themselves will be able to start breeding.

In captivity, the breeding of cheetahs proved impossible until recently. The first successful breeding in a zoo did not take place until 1960, in Germany. This is despite the fact that there have been captive cheetahs, used as hunting companions by royal princes and powerful rulers, for over five thousand years. All those early "companion" cheetahs had to be caught in the wild and tamed.

Season after season, in ancient times, cheetahs were trapped and trained, then taken out on royal hunts to chase antelope or other prey. They were hooded like eagles until the last moment then, when the prey was sighted, the hoods were quickly removed and the "hunting leopards," as they were incorrectly called, were allowed to charge after their fleeing victims.

If each ruler or prince had taken only one or two cheetahs for use on the hunt, there would have been little to worry about. But rulers are often greedy and want to show off to their friends and rivals. Because of this, they kept huge stables full of wild-caught cheetahs, each man wanting to outdo the others. One great ruler boasted that he kept no fewer than a thousand cheetahs at one time in his magnificent stables. No wonder the cheetah numbers have fallen so much over the centuries.

Cheetahs used to be a common sight on the open plains of Africa, the Middle East and parts of Asia, but today there are very few left. It is over forty years since a wild one was spotted in India and the chances are that they have all now vanished for good from that continent. The final moment for the Indian cheetah was a sad one. One dark night a local ruler was driving his car along a country road when he spotted

three of these beautiful cats, dazzled by his headlights. He calmly stopped his car, got out and shot them. India was to see no more.

In the Middle East and western Asia it is also nearly extinct, but there are probably a few still hanging on in the most remote areas, where human beings seldom set foot. In Africa it can still be seen by anyone taking a holiday safari in the game parks. Even there, though, it is becoming less and less common.

The African cheetah's problem today is not that it is being hunted, but that it is too popular. Every visitor to Africa wants to see these beautiful cats. To please their guests, the guides spend hours driving around in their minibuses looking for them. As soon as they see one, they follow it as closely as possible, while the tourists take photographs from the bus windows. If the cheetahs are resting, this creates no difficulties, but if they are hunting they are easily disturbed.

The situation is getting worse. There are so few cheetahs and so many tourists, that in some areas the animals are quite unable to catch and kill their prey because, from dawn to dusk, the minibuses never leave them alone. The human visitors mean them no harm, but it is they, rather than hunters, who are now causing the disappearance of the cheetah from its old haunts on the plains of Africa.

At the last count there were 25,000 cheetahs left in the whole of Africa. This may sound like a huge number, but remembering what a vast continent it is, the figure is not so impressive. We must make sure it does not fall any lower.

# The Sea Lion

BACK IN THE DAYS WHEN PERFORMING ANIMALS WERE STILL POPULAR at the circus, sea lions were among the favorites. They played musical instruments by blowing into them, balanced beach-balls on the tips of their noses and clapped the audience by slapping their flippers together. People were amazed by their intelligence and their acrobatics.

The reason why circus-goers were so surprised by the skills of the performing sea lions was that, at first sight, the animals seemed so clumsy. They waddled awkwardly into the circus ring on their flippers, heaving their heavy bodies along as best they could. Children laughed at them because they seemed so helpless. Then, suddenly, these great, blubbery bodies were performing their act with delicate, graceful movements. The contrast was astonishing. It was like watching a big wrestler performing as a ballet dancer. What was the explanation?

To find the answer we have to study sea lions, not on dry land, but in the sea. There, it is not hard to discover their secret. Once in the water, their bodies, so awkward on land, become immensely skillful and athletic.

When they chase a shoal of fish, the twists and turns of the sea lions' necks are so fast and so sensitive that it becomes easy to understand their success at balancing a ball on their nose. As the fish dart this way and that, trying to avoid being caught in their jaws, the sea lions must follow their movements at lightning speed if they are to catch their prey. And catch them they do — large numbers of them every day. An adult sea lion can gobble up as much as 40 pounds of fish every twenty-four hours.

These intelligent, playful, inquisitive hunters did not always live in the sea. Their ancestors were land animals. At some point, millions of years ago, they returned to the water and their bodies changed shape. Their legs became flippers, they became streamlined and they developed a thick layer of blubber. Today they have about 4 inches of blubber beneath their short, smooth coat of fur. This fat acts like a heavy overcoat, helping to keep them warm in the sea. Without it they would soon die of cold.

One of the problems of being covered in blubber is that, although it keeps the cold out, it can also make it difficult to lose heat in warm weather. Most members of the seal family live in the colder waters of the world, and do not have to face a problem of over-heating, but a few, like the Californian sea lion, make their homes in a hotter climate. For them, there has to be some special way of avoiding over-heating.

The answer lies in their flippers. These are covered in large areas of naked skin. There are many blood vessels just beneath the surface and the seals are able to increase or decrease the flow of blood through these vessels. The more hot blood that passes close to the skin surface, the more heat is lost, and the more quickly the sea lion can cool down. One of the strangest sights is to see a family of sea lions, all lying in the sea together, with their flippers sticking out of the water. As the breezes blow on them, these "sails" are flapped about in the air to increase the cooling.

All members of the seal family have developed special valves that can close off their nostrils. This happens automatically every time the seal or sea lion dives. Also the tongue can be moved up to block off the passage at the back of the throat. This means that when the animal is swimming under water it can open its mouth and use its sharp teeth to catch fish, without any danger of swallowing seawater or choking.

Sea lions and seals are very closely related, but it is easy to tell them apart. Sea lions have small ears sticking out at the sides of the head. Seals have completely streamlined ears, with just a small hole showing at the sides of the head. On land, sea lions can twist their hind flippers forwards and use them as short legs when walking. Seals cannot do this and can only drag themselves along with their front flippers, bouncing their fat bodies on the rocks in a most uncomfortable way.

Sea lions can hold their breath for about five minutes, but they dive so well and so quickly that, even in a short space of time, they can get down to depths of almost 200 feet. Some other members of the seal family can do much better than this, staying down for ten times as long and diving ten times deeper. But although these other seals may be better in the sea, the sea lion has the advantage on land, where its better locomotion enables it to gallop clumsily around the beaches when it comes ashore.

Unlike whales and dolphins, all seals and sea lions have to breed on land. Each spring, when the mating season arrives, the male sea lions gather on a patch of land. Their barking, honking cries can be heard from far away. Each male tries to defend what he considers to be the best part of the beach.

Eventually the males are all spaced out down the shoreline, waiting for the appearance of the females. Arriving late, all the females are heavily pregnant when they come ashore. Every male tries to gather together as many as he can. Top males usually manage to build up a harem of about twenty, and they must then protect these from the rival bulls. This involves a great deal more calling, displaying and threatening. Fights break out again and again and the bulls are often badly injured. They have thicker, heavier necks than the females and this extra fat helps to reduce the damage done by the powerful jaws of the rival males. It is not uncommon to see a weary warrior with terrible gashes and blood pouring down his body.

Soon after they come ashore, the females give birth. Each one has a single calf and the newborn are soon feeding contentedly on their mother's milk. Life for them is not too peaceful, however, because the big males are repeatedly charging back and forth during their battles and sometimes trample a baby sea lion to death beneath their great weight. The bulls are so much bigger than the cows that there is little the mothers can do to save their young. However, most survive and after they have been weaned, take to the sea for the first time.

Meanwhile, their mothers will have mated again with the big bulls, and soon they all depart to spend the rest of the year feeding. The young animals follow their mothers for about a year. Life is easy for them, with plenty of fish to eat. Other food, such as octopus, squid and the occasional seabird, is always there to add variety.

There are six different kinds of sea lions alive today, all closely related. The one we know best is the Californian sea lion, which lives all down the west coast of North America. There are 50,000 of these. Then there is its relative, the Galapagos sea lion, found only around the Galapagos Islands in the middle of the Pacific Ocean. There are only 40,000 of those.

The two rarest ones are the New Zealand sea lion – only 4,000 remaining – and the Australian sea lion – even fewer, only 3,000 left. The two most common ones are the South American sea lion, of which there are 270,000, and the Steller's sea lion from the north Pacific, of which there are 250,000. With so many other large animals under threat from man, it is good to be able to report that the sea lions, at least, are holding their own in our modern world.

# The Zebra

THE ZEBRA IS THE WILD HORSE OF AFRICA. IT MAY LOOK VERY DIFFERENT from our familiar, domesticated horses, but beneath its beautiful skin, it is much the same kind of animal as the one we see in the stableyard or on the racetrack.

Apart from its striped coat, it differs from the domestic horse in only one important respect: it is much more difficult to tame. The horse is a friendly co-operative creature, easy to convert into "man's best slave." The zebra is far less docile and has always refused to allow any human being to ride on its back. When a film was being made in Africa about a "jungle princess" this posed a problem, because in the story she was supposed to travel everywhere on the back of her tame zebra. No such animal could be found and so the film company had to hire a girl with a white horse and persuade her to paint it very carefully with black stripes.

Because they have never been domesticated, the only place today where you can see large numbers of zebras is on the grassy plains of tropical Africa, their original homeland. There they live in small groups each containing a powerful male, his harem of females and their young. The male has to spend a great deal of his energy controlling his little band and making sure that they do not stray.

Watching from a respectful distance are the other, less successful males. These cluster together in all-male groups and wait for the day when they themselves may be strong enough to win a harem of females. From time to time, one of these young stallions will risk challenging an older male to a fight. If he wins, he will be able to drive the older one away and take over his harem.

Another way in which a stallion can become a harem-master is to wait until the younger females have reached the age when they feel the urge to wander. This happens when they are about to become adults. Instead of staying with their parents, both the young males and the young females leave their family group and drift away. The nearby bachelor stallions watch these movements intently and quickly move in to round up as many young females as they can control. In this way new groups are formed and will soon be breeding in their turn.

Like horses, zebras nearly always give birth to single foals. Twins are extremely rare. When the mare is about to give birth, she finds the quietest spot she can. If she is at all uneasy or agitated, she delays giving birth. She is capable of doing this for several days if necessary, until she feels it is just the right moment. Only then will she allow her foal to be thrust into the harsh, outside world. If she was not able to time her act of birth in this way, her newborn would be much more likely to fall prey to waiting killers.

When it appears, the little zebra foal has no time to lose. With hungry killers always on the prowl, it cannot afford to lie weakly on the ground for very long. Within ten minutes it is up on its feet and is soon feeding from its mother. Its spindly legs seem to grow stronger by the second. Only half an hour after its birth it is ready to start trotting along with the herd.

When the group is resting, the mother will lick her new arrival repeatedly and in this way will learn its individual smell. At the same time the foal will be getting to know the particular smell of its mother. In no time they will be able to identify one another and a strong bond of love will have grown between them.

As the days pass, the young zebra will come to recognize all the members of its herd, not only by their personal smell, but also by the details of their black and white stripes. Every zebra has its own special pattern and, just as with human fingerprints, no two are exactly alike.

As it grows older, the foal's biggest problem will be keeping up with the group. Its mother will feed it and protect it as best she can, but if the group has to flee from lions or packs of wild dogs, the newcomer's legs may not be fast enough to carry it to safety. If the group scatters in panic, the foal may become cut off on its own. If that happens it will be at serious risk, and many zebras are killed before they become fully grown adults.

Once the herd has scattered and the hunters have gone, the zebras start calling out to one another with a special cry. Each animal has its own personal call and the others can recognize its voice, so they can soon get back together again as a family group.

This means that zebras have three ways of recognizing one another: by body-smell, by stripe-pattern and by voice. Smell can be used when they are in close contact, or at night-time. Stripes can be used when they are not too far apart. And voice can be used when they are a long way from one another. Having these three different ways of keeping in touch is a great help to an animal that must always live in family groups if it is to survive.

Sometimes, zebras are bold. They do not always flee when they are attacked by killers. If the mare sees her foal being attacked, she may become suddenly very fierce and fearless, and her stallion may also become aggressive. Experienced lions know this may happen, and take steps to protect themselves, but young lions on their first hunts are not always prepared for the zebras' anger. Sometimes the big cats are badly injured by the savage kicking of the furious herd. It is said that on one occasion, zebras even attacked a man. A poacher who had killed a zebra foal was kicked and bitten to death by its family.

Within a year the young zebra will be able to look after itself and will no longer be feeding from its mother. If it is a female it will remain with its family for about another year, before drifting away. Young males stay a little longer with their original families, often reaching the age of four before they depart to join the nearby bachelor groups.

When they reach the age of about seven, these young males will start to challenge the old stallions, trying to drive them away from their harems. If the males are getting old – around the age of eighteen years – they may no longer be strong enough to win the fight and may have to leave for a sad, solitary old age. If they are

still in their prime, though, they will quickly send the younger males packing.

The daily routine of the herd varies with the weather. If it is raining, they move about very little and usually keep to their sleeping area. If it is a fine day, they set off at dawn in single file, leaving the sleeping place behind them. They then eat, drink and rest, eat, drink and rest, through the remainder of the day. In the late afternoon they trek back once more to their favorite sleeping spot, where they pass the hours of darkness. During the night they have three main sleep periods, with short "grazing snacks" in between them.

If there is a drought and the water-holes dry up, all this changes. Unlike camels, the zebras cannot go for very long without drinking. If they cannot find water within three days, they are in serious trouble. So, when the dry season comes, the little family groups join up into a vast gathering of hundreds of animals and together they travel to wetter country. This may mean that they have to migrate for many miles, but they are strong, sturdy animals and can journey for hour after hour without tiring.

During moments of rest, the zebra spends a great deal of time keeping itself clean. It uses many different actions to do this. It may suck or nibble its skin. It may quiver its flesh to frighten off flies and it can also swish them away with its long tail. It can also drive them away from its legs by stamping its foot hard on the ground. It can scratch itself with its hind leg, rather like a dog. If it has an irritation, it can rub itself up against a tree-trunk or a branch. If its back is itching, it can throw itself down on the ground and roll over on the earth, or on a patch of sandy soil.

If one zebra is resting near to another, the two animals will often stand head to tail. They can then swish the flies off one another's faces. Or they may stand head to head and nibble one another's necks and manes — places that they themselves cannot reach.

The one great mystery about zebras is why they should have such vivid black and white coats. Everyone used to say that the stripes helped to hide the zebras from their enemies, but this is not true. If you visit Africa it does not take long to see how easy it is to spot a group of zebras. Their stripes really do not hide them at all. There has to be some other reason for having stripes, but nobody can agree what it is.

Some people think that the black and white markings dazzle the lions as they attack, making the hunters miss their prey as they pounce. Others believe that, when the zebras are fleeing together in a herd, the stripes make it difficult to see where one animal ends and another begins. Because of this it is thought that an attacking lion finds it difficult to pick one victim out from the rest.

Another idea is that the stripes help the animals that wear them to tell one kind of zebra from another. There are three main types alive today — the common plains zebra which lives on the grasslands of most of East Africa, the rare Grevy's zebra found further north, and the very rare mountain zebra down in the south. Could it be that the different patterns of stripes act like flags on a battlefield, telling the animals where their own "troops" are to be found? This does not seem very likely because at a distance the stripes all look much the same. You have to get close to spot the

COMMON             GREVY'S             MOUNTAIN

differences, and by then you can identify each animal personally.

Only on one part of their bodies do zebras have what could be called "flags," and that is on their rumps. On this part of the coat the stripes differ strongly. The common zebra has bold lines, the Grevy's zebra has a strange white patch with a central black mark, and the mountain zebra has a gridiron pattern of fine lines. It is no accident that this is just the part of the zebra that is most visible when it is running away. This makes it easier for a fleeing zebra to keep with its own kind and prevents it from rushing off in panic with the wrong herd.

A completely different idea about the stripes suggests that they are really there to prevent stinging insects from landing on the animal's skin and biting it. It is thought that some insects hate alighting on such a vivid pattern of black and white and go off, instead, to worry some other victim. If this is true, it would explain why zebras are so healthy and successful in tropical Africa. Domestic horses, taken there by man, have often suffered from diseases that the zebras seem to avoid. Perhaps it is the stripes that are protecting them.

There are several other suggestions as to why zebras have stripes, but even today nobody is certain which is the true explanation. It is a mystery that remains to be solved by some young zoologist in the years to come.

# The Camel

THE CAMEL IS THE ONLY REALLY BIG ANIMAL THAT CAN SURVIVE WELL IN the burning heat of the desert. The smaller desert creatures, like the rats and mice, can avoid the heat of the day by hiding in burrows below the surface. They only need to come up at night, when it is wonderfully cool. They can then move about in comfort. But the huge body of the camel must be able to stand up to the intense glare of the sun, for hour after hour, every day. How does it manage to do this?

Everyone knows that the camel has a hump and many people believe that this hump contains a supply of stored water. The idea is that, when the camel gets hotter and hotter as the sun rises in the sky, it can use its secret water supply to quench its thirst. Although this story has been told for many years, it is simply not true. The camel does not have a special water-supply in its hump or anywhere else. It manages to avoid over-heating in a completely different way.

The true secret of the hump is that it acts as a barrier, reducing the damage done by the hot sun beating down from above. It contains a great deal of fat, and this fat is very bad at allowing heat to pass though it. So the more delicate organs inside the camel's body are protected by this "heat shield" that rests on top of the animal's back.

This also explains why the camel's body is so slender, when you look at it from the front or from behind. Its narrow, upright shape means that it exposes far less of its surface to the sun's rays at midday, when the sun is directly above the animal and is at its hottest.

If the camel had its fat spread out all over its body, like so many other animals, instead of heaped up in a large hump on its back, the cooling would be lost. Instead of acting like a sun-hat, its fat would be more like a heavy, wrap-around overcoat. Instead of helping to lower the body temperature, it would increase it.

In addition to acting as a sun-shield, the fat inside the hump also provides an extra food supply when times are hard. Many different kinds of animals build up layers of fat beneath the skin when feeding is easy, and then use this up when food is scarce. Having a lot of fat is like having a portable larder that you can raid when you need emergency rations.

Because the desert sun is so incredibly hot, with temperatures sometimes rising above 50°C, (or more than 120°F), the camel needs more than just a hump and a slender body to protect it. Its second secret is that it can vary its body temperature without suffering any ill-effects.

If you have ever been in bed with a fever you will know that when your temperature rises to over 100°F, you start to feel horribly ill. Humans can stand only very small changes in body temperature without suffering uncomfortably. The camel has somehow managed to overcome this. During the hot day it can allow its body to heat up to an astonishing 101°F, without even breaking into a sweat. During the cold night it can let its body cool down to as little as 95°F, without suffering from a chill.

This ability means that the camel's body can accept more and more heat during the day and lose it during the night. Then, in the morning, it is ready to face being heated up all over again.

If it could not do this it would have to keep cool like other animals, by panting and sweating. But panting and sweating both involve loss of water and this is something the camel cannot afford. The desert is not only very hot, it is also very dry, and camels must sometimes go for days without a drink as they trek across the barren, sandy wastelands. They must avoid any water loss, if they are to stay alive. If they cooled themselves like we do, by pouring with sweat, they would quickly dry up, shrivel and collapse.

When it is crossing a desert, it is so important for a camel to lose as little water as possible that it cannot even allow itself to produce any urine. Passing urine is important because it means getting rid of waste matter from the body, but it also involves a heavy water loss because the waste has to be literally washed away from the body. This is a water loss the camel cannot afford and it has to get rid of its waste in a special way. When it becomes intensely hot, it can by-pass its kidneys and send all its waste matter through its stomach instead. In this way it can get rid of all the dangerous chemicals in its body as dry droppings, and avoid passing urine almost entirely.

When camels do manage to reach a precious pool of water, at an oasis, they drink greedily and can take in 20 gallons in a matter of a few minutes. This is about the same amount of liquid that it takes to fill up the gas tank of a Rolls-Royce, but there is a difference. The Rolls could only travel for about a day with one such filling, but the camel can journey for over two weeks before getting its next drink. The camel is indeed the Rolls-Royce of the desert.

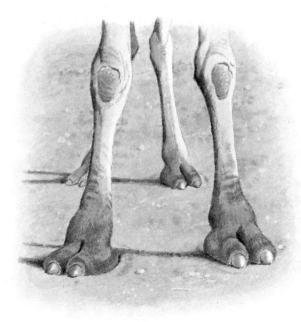

Moving through desert country has a third problem. It is not only very hot and very dry, the ground is also very soft. The shifting sands make it hard to walk. Horses quickly tire on sandy wastes. What is needed is a special kind of foot – big, flat and soft – and that is yet another of the camel's special features. With their huge feet plodding across the vast desert wastes, they made it possible for ancient peoples to set up new trade routes all over the Middle East and played a vital role in the growth of early civilizations.

Despite the brilliant way in which the camel's body can deal with the difficulties of desert living, it has hardly ever been looked upon as a noble animal, like the horse. In fact, many people have expressed disgust when encountering the camel for the first time. It has often been described as smelly, noisy, stubborn, stupid and ugly. This is very unfair to a magnificent animal that is capable of such amazing feats of survival.

It is true that it is smelly, but even that quality has been put to good use in warfare. In ancient battles it was discovered that a troop of camels could terrify and scatter a troop of horses, simply because the horses could not stand their odor.

It is also true that the camel is noisy and stubborn, but that is simply because, unlike the docile horse, it does not take kindly to being trained and controlled by man. And it is only their reluctance to carry out quickly every task their owners give them that makes them seem stupid.

As for their being ugly, this is a matter of opinion. Seen in a zoo or a circus they may not look at their best, but on the sands of the desert, striding elegantly along, they have a dramatic style all of their own.

Also, if you look at the camel closely enough, you will find that it has an extraordinary face. Although some people find it unpleasant, even its worst critic would have to admit that it does have the most beautiful eyelashes in the whole of the animal kingdom. This is no accident, because the camel's eyes need special protection in the desert, where sand is often being blown about by high winds and there can sometimes be severe sand-storms. Then, the huge lashes act as a curtain, shielding the delicate surfaces of the eyes from harm.

Another protection from sand-storms is the camel's ability to shut its nostrils tight. When they are fully open they reveal huge nasal cavities, but when sand is blowing through the air, special valves close them down to slits, sealing the cavities off from the outside world.

Beneath the big nostrils are the huge, rubbery lips. The upper lip is split into two halves and the mouth is very flexible, making it possible for the camel to browse on very harsh and often prickly vegetation. It can feed on bushes and shrubs that no other animal would try to tackle. Its long, curved neck enables it to reach out in search of even the tiniest leaf or shoot.

The social life of the camel is only known from the behavior of tame camels that have gone wild and started to fend for themselves in remote areas. These animals form into small herds each of which consists of a dominant male and between six and twenty females. The weaker males form separate bachelor groups and keep to themselves until one of them feels bold enough to challenge the herd-master. Then a serious fight can take place, with each male trying to make himself look as fierce as possible.

As the fight begins, the short tail is swished and the neck is lowered and then raised. As this occurs, something quite extraordinary happens. Drooling and gobbling, the males blow up the insides of their mouths like great rubber balloons. Their mouths literally turn inside out and the big rubbery balloons of flesh hang down and out of their mouths in a startling threat display. The balloon is known as a "goulla," because this is the kind of gobbling noise that the displaying animals make.

Eventually one camel attacks the other, biting at the opponent's legs and especially his neck. The main aim is to hold the enemy's neck down with the camel's own neck, and keep it pressed to the ground. If successful, this soon forces the rival's whole body down on to the earth, where it is squashed under the weight of the triumphant winner.

It used to be a common sight in Turkey to see natural camel-fighting of this kind turned into an organized spectacle. But the cruelty of this so-called sport led to it being outlawed back in 1967.

There are two kinds of camels alive today. They are the thick-coated Bactrian camel from the deserts of central Asia, which has two humps, and the more slender Arabian camel from the deserts of North Africa and the Middle East, which has only one hump. If you are asked to ride a camel, it is always a good idea to enquire "One hump or two?," because it is much easier to sit in between the two humps of the Bactrian than to perch on top of the single hump of the Arabian.

Despite this, it is the Arabian that has been mastered as a racing animal. The "thoroughbred" racing camel is known as a dromedary and the speeds it can reach are astonishing. Over long distances, it can out-pace even the fastest racehorse. The jockeys are usually very young boys, whose small bodies are better at staying in the saddle when the animals are at full gallop.

Camels were first domesticated about six thousand years ago. Their main use has always been for carrying heavy burdens over long distances, but they have also frequently been ridden and even harnessed to the plough and put to work tilling the fields.

Despite the later arrival of machines for transport and for farm work, camels have not become rare animals. Although nearly all the truly wild ones have vanished, there are still huge numbers of domesticated camels and many of those have escaped to form wandering herds.

It is thought that there are altogether about 14 million domesticated camels alive in the world today. Of these, about 90 percent are the one-humped, Arabian camels. They are common in North Africa, the Middle East, Asia and in certain parts of Australia. One day they will probably all be replaced by modern machinery, but for the present these tough, long-suffering beasts can still be seen slowly, and sometimes with noisy complaints, carrying out their various tasks and duties. For the modern tourist they are a novelty, but for many of the people living in difficult desert lands, they remain a vital and sometimes life-saving servant, regularly capable of traveling 12 miles a day, for week after week and month after month.

Truly, the camel has been well named as the "ship of the desert."

# The Chimpanzee

O F ALL OUR ANIMAL RELATIVES, THE CHIMPANZEE IS THE MOST INTELLIGENT. Give a chimpanzee a new problem and it will solve it quicker than any other ape or monkey. It is so similar to us that, for some people, it is too close for comfort. They find its cleverness alarming because they are reminded of just how close we really are to our animal relations. But they should not be worried by this because, if we like and respect animals, we should be proud to consider ourselves their cousins.

So what kind of animal is our closest relative? Chimps live in the tropical forests of West Africa. There they spend much of the day wandering around, searching for food. Most of the time they walk along on all fours, using the knuckles of their hands, rather than their palms. Baby chimps cling on to their mothers' bodies when the group is on the move. Older infants hitch a ride on their mothers' backs.

At the first sign of danger, the animals take to the trees, clambering up to safety and then staring down at the ground to watch for trouble. If a killer, such as a leopard, is seen approaching, they may flee through the trees, or they may mob it by screaming, hooting and breaking off branches which fall to the ground and frighten the killer away.

When peace returns they clamber back down to the ground and continue their search for ripe fruits. If they find a fruit tree in perfect condition, they will spend a long time lingering there, gorging themselves on the sweet, juicy food. Altogether fruit-eating takes up about one third of their day. They always eat what they find on the spot and never make food stores or larders. This is because food of some kind or other is always available to them.

Chimps enjoy a wide variety of foods. In addition to the four hours of fruit-eating every day, they spend two hours munching on succulent young leaves and shoots. They also take seeds, nuts, flowers and even bark. Their daily diet includes about two dozen different types of food. During the course of a year they will feed on several hundred different kinds of vegetation.

For a long while it was thought that chimps only ate plant foods, but we now know that this is not true. They also search for insects of many kinds, especially termites. They fish for these with thin sticks that they push into termite hills. The termites inside, angry at the stick prodding them, bite it with their jaws and cling on to it. The ape then pulls the stick out and wipes it swiftly through its lips. The termites are brushed off the stick, into the animal's mouth, and are neatly swallowed.

When they are feeding in this way, the chimps first select a suitable stick, then they improve it by breaking off any small side-branches. This means that they are not only tool-users, but tool-makers. Some years ago it was said that man was *the* tool-maker and this separated him from the other animals. We can no longer claim this difference.

In the last few years it has been discovered that, once in a while, chimpanzees will also hunt, kill and eat quite large prey animals. They have been known to attack monkeys, pigs and even small antelopes. A group of apes sets off in search of a victim and behaves very much like a group of primitive human hunters. Some apes drive the prey, others corner and kill it. The body is quickly torn to pieces and the strongest apes sit around and eat the meat. If they have close friends, they will share a little of the meat with them. Others may beg with outstretched hands, but they are ignored. Perhaps because hunting is not one of the main activities of chimps they do not carry out the full food-sharing that is found among some of the carnivores, such as wolves and wild hunting dogs.

Another new discovery is that wild chimpanzees have invented far more tools than we knew about in the past. In some regions they employ no fewer than seventeen different kinds. To give just a few examples: they have been seen to use fly-whisks to get rid of pests, large leaves as toilet-paper, and hammers and anvils to crack open hard shells. They have thrown rocks as missiles when hunting, hurled sticks when defending themselves against enemies, and squeezed water from sponges of chewed-up bark when drinking. For sheer cleverness there is nothing in the forest to touch them.

When they are not feeding, the group of chimpanzees rests in a clearing and relaxes for a while. This is the moment for grooming, snoozing and play. It is vital for these animals to keep their fur and skin in good condition and they spend a great deal of time examining their own bodies and those of their companions. Grooming one another is an important social activity. It makes it possible to keep clean those parts of the body that an animal cannot reach with its own hands, and it also helps to make friendly relations between the chimps much stronger.

While the adults are resting, the young apes play nearby. If they are very young, their mothers keep a close eye on them, making sure that they do not stray too far and do not get bullied or hurt themselves.

Chimp play is very energetic, involving chasing, wrestling, mock fighting, and all kinds of acrobatics. The animals have a special "play-face" – an expression that says "I am not serious" when they attack one another. The mouth is open, but the lips are stretched to cover the teeth. At the same time they make soft grunting noises. This is their chimp version of our human smiling and laughing. It is important for them because it prevents any play-fighting from being mistaken for real fighting. Next to human beings, the chimpanzee has the most expressive face in the animal world.

When evening comes, the chimps climb into the trees and settle down there for the night. Unlike monkeys, though, they do not simply sit on a branch and go to sleep. Instead, they make themselves a special bed on which to lie down. They do this by pulling small branches towards themselves one by one, bending them over or breaking them off and creating a mattress of twigs and leaves. When it feels right, they stretch out on it and test it. If it is not springy or soft enough, they get up again and search for more leaves to improve it. At last, they are content and go to sleep.

Each baby chimp sleeps with its mother, clinging to her fur and with her large arms enfolding its small body. Mothers have only one baby at a time, and it will be allowed to share her bed and feed on her milk until, after about three years, she has a new baby to care for. Even then, though, when the new baby has arrived and is the center of attention, the older infant will remain close to its mother. She will continue to care for it and protect it for several more years. Childhood lasts a long time for chimpanzees and the young animals will not start breeding until they are about ten years old.

The great mystery surrounding the chimpanzee today is why it has such a large brain. Why does it need to be so intelligent? Other monkeys, with much smaller

RELAXED                                      HOOTING

AGGRESSIVE                                   PLAYFUL

brains, enjoy the same sort of lifestyle, searching for fruits, nuts and seeds, living in a social group, grooming one another's fur and playing in much the same way when they are young. It is hard to see why the chimpanzee became quite so brainy.

In captivity we know just how bright chimps can be, if encouraged to express themselves in certain ways. They can, for instance, be taught to work complicated machines. They can also learn simple sign language, so that people can "talk" to them with hand signals. They have even been able to paint simple pictures, carefully placing the lines on the paper in exactly the pattern they want. So far they have not been able to paint a picture of anything that we can recognize, but their simple scribbles do show that they have the ability to arrange patterns, balance designs and keep to a given space. It is quite wrong to suggest that these apes have "language" or are "artists" in the human sense, but it is clear that they are almost there.

These discoveries tell us that the chimpanzee has a wonderful brain, but it does not seem to make much use of it in its daily life, apart from inventing various simple tools.

One fascinating idea that has been suggested is that chimps were once much more like humans in their behavior, but have long since returned to a more monkey-like way of living in the tropical forests. Perhaps their ancestors competed with early human hunters, lost the struggle and retreated into the forests? We humans then went on to conquer the world, while the apes stayed safely hidden away in their forest strongholds. There they had few enemies and were able to enjoy a simpler lifestyle.

This lifestyle is now, for the first time, under serious threat because of the huge numbers of humans living in tropical Africa. The growing human population is spreading more and more into the forest regions, cutting down the trees and using the land for farming. There are thought to be more than 50,000 chimpanzees left, but the number is getting smaller each year. It is not yet a rare animal, but could easily become one in a few decades if the growth of farming is allowed to continue without any checks. It would be very sad if our closest living relative were to vanish.

# The Armadillo

FOR ANY ANIMAL, THE GREATEST CHALLENGE IS HOW TO AVOID BECOMING a tasty meal. Wherever it lives there will always be hungry predators on the prowl and, against these, it must have some form of defence.

For certain animals, the solution is hiding, so that they cannot be seen. For others, it is fast fleeing, so that they cannot be caught. For still others, it is to fight back, with sharp spines, savage teeth, or deadly poison.

In addition to these three basic defences, there is a fourth: armor. Many animals protect themselves by wearing a hard outer shell like a suit of knight's armor and, as their name suggests, this is the solution of those fascinating South American animals, the armadillos.

The bony shell of an armadillo is so tough that few killers can crack it with their teeth. Even the most powerful of the South American flesh-eaters usually prefer to look elsewhere for an evening snack.

For an animal seeking a safe and simple way of life, this may seem like a perfect solution. There is, however, one big drawback to being armored. The body becomes stiff and rather rigid. Movements are slow and cumbersome. This sets the heavily armored creatures apart from other animals.

The wonderfully fluid actions of soft-furred animals mean that they can be athletic in everything they do. They can escape more easily from natural disasters, like forest fires and floods. They can move more quickly to new homes when food runs out. They can climb, leap, glide or fly with ease.

By contrast, the armored animal must make do with a clumsy lifestyle. What it gains in body protection, it loses in body freedom.

How does the armadillo deal with this problem? One way is to become less rigid. Without losing the protection of the hard shell, the animal can become more agile by having jointed armour, so that it can bend its body a little. The armadillo does this by having several hinges, or bands, across its mid-section. By opening and closing them, it can roll itself up or flatten itself out.

Unlike the tortoises and turtles, which have fixed shells, all in one large piece, the shells of the armadillos are separated by these bands into two smaller sections — the front, or shoulder-shield, and the rear, or rump-shield.

This design of armor makes them look like mechanical toys. When you see an armadillo for the first time, you feel you want to wind it up with a key to watch it run.

The different kinds of armadillos have different numbers of hinges, or bands. Some of them are actually named by their bands, like the three-banded, the six-banded and the nine-banded armadillos.

Because they can unbend their shells with these hinges, the little armadillos are capable of running quite well on their short legs. They can never reach the sort of speeds that would be needed to escape a quick hunter, but if they can hear trouble coming from a long way off, they do at least have the chance to make for cover. Once in the undergrowth, their hard shells give them the great advantage of being able to push through prickly, scratchy bushes and plants without being hurt. The killer on their trail may think twice before trying to follow them.

Scampering away, the retreating armadillos make for the safety of their burrows. If there is no burrow nearby, they will start to dig on the spot. Scrabbling away with their front feet and kicking the earth backwards behind them, they go on digging until they are completely hidden beneath the surface, or until only the hard, bony shells of their backs are visible. Then they pause and wait for the danger to pass.

If they are found when they are half-buried, they are difficult to dislodge. They jam themselves in as tight as possible and stay very still. All the hunter can see is their smooth, hard, rounded back. There is nothing to grip on to, no matter how wide the hungry jaws may open.

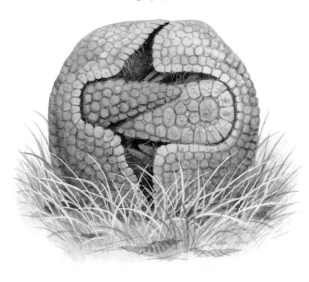

If their enemy reaches them before they can dig in, they must rely solely on their armor to save them. Some kinds of armadillo are capable of rolling up into such a tight ball that all their soft parts can be completely hidden from view, even without digging down into the earth. The three-banded armadillo can turn itself into an almost perfect sphere when it is attacked. Looking like a giant woodlouse, it curls its shell round and plugs the gap, where the two ends meet, with its head and its tail. Only the top of its head and tail can be seen, and both of these are covered in a heavy plate of armor.

This seems the perfect way for an armadillo to protect itself, because no killers can get their jaws around the bony ball. No matter how hard they bite at it, their teeth keep slipping off the tough surface. Eventually they give up and wander away in search of an easier victim. After a long wait, making sure that all is quiet at last, the little armadillo uncurls itself, looks around, and then scurries off to safety.

There have been moments, though, when this method of self-defence has misfired badly. On one occasion, a human hunter was out walking along a path on a hillside in South America. A family of three-banded armadillos was trotting quietly along in his direction, higher up the hill. When they saw the hunter they all quickly curled themselves up into tight balls. Because of the slope of the hill they then rolled down and down, until they came to rest on the path at the hunter's feet. He promptly bent down, picked them up, popped them into his collecting bag, and strolled on with the easiest catch of the day.

If an armadillo comes to a stretch of water, it may be in difficulty. Its suit of armor makes it amazingly heavy for its small size and if it wants to swim it has to protect itself from sinking. One kind of armadillo is known to do this in a remarkable way. Before it takes to the water, it breathes deeply and fills its body with air. You might say that this is no more strange than a human swimmer taking a deep breath before jumping into a swimming pool, but there is a special difference. When the armadillo does it, it not only fills its lungs with air, but also its stomach and its intestines. This makes it float like a balloon and it can then swim safely on the surface of the water.

To move through the water like this, the armadillo must, of course, hold its breath. If it were to breathe out, it would sink like a stone. So it cannot swim for very long. But here again this strange animal has a surprise for us, for it can hold its breath for as long as six minutes. This gives it plenty of time to cross a river or swim to safety.

It uses this same breath-holding trick when it is feeding. It hunts for almost any small creatures that live in the soil, especially insects. Guided by its sense of smell, it can detect the presence of its prey down to a depth of 8 inches. Scratching frantically with its front feet, it keeps its nose thrust into the ground, trying to sniff anything that might be hiding there. During this search for food it must once again hold its breath for long periods, or it will find itself repeatedly choking on a cloud of dust.

Today there are twenty species of armadillos still surviving in South America. They range from the impressive giant armadillo, which is just over 3 feet long, right down to the tiny fairy armadillo that measures no more than 5 inches.

The most successful of them is the nine-banded armadillo, which is found as far south as Argentina and right up into Central America. It even reaches the southern areas of the United States, where large numbers are killed on the roads at night. Because it destroys so many insect pests, it is looked upon as a friend by local farmers and generally left in peace. It has even been deliberately introduced into certain areas in Florida and other southern states, as a natural pest-controller.

One of the strangest facts about the nine-banded armadillo is that it always gives birth to quadruplets. Every time a female becomes a mother she produces either four identical little males or identical little females. No male ever has a sister and no female ever has a brother.

Some other species of armadillo are also known to have quads, but one goes even further, producing eight or even twelve babies, again with all the members of a particular litter having the same sex.

Perhaps the most surprising fact of all, though, is that some of the prehistoric ancestors of our modern armadillos were as big as a rhinoceros. They were so large that their shells were used as roofs for the homes of the earliest humans to arrive on the American continent. A single shell could be almost 10 feet long, dwarfing that of the present-day "giant" armadillo. Scooped out, dried and turned upside down, it provided a ready-made cover for the primitive huts of the first Indians.

Today's armadillos are far too small to be any use in hut-building, but in some regions there is a popular trade in armadillo bowls and baskets. These are made from their dried shells, with a handle made by tying the head to the tail. In certain parts of South America, their shells are also used as sound-boxes for native musical instruments. This means that many of these delightful creatures are killed to make a few dollars out of visiting tourists who are searching for local novelties. For such harmless, pest-eating animals, this seems an unkind fate.

# The Platypus

I F THERE WAS A PRIZE FOR THE STRANGEST ANIMAL IN THE WORLD, THE platypus would be the easy winner. This amazing mammal from the rivers of Australia looks as though it has been put together using spare parts from other animals. It seems to have the bill of a duck, the body of an otter and the tail of a beaver.

When the stuffed body of one was first brought to Europe, people were convinced that it was a fake. They were sure that, for a joke, someone in Australia had glued together these different parts and was trying to pass them off as some weird new kind of animal.

We now know that the platypus is a perfectly genuine animal, but it is not difficult to see why it was doubted by those experts who first set eyes on its dead body, about two hundred years ago. Practical jokers had been trying to play tricks on museums for a long time, and the staff were naturally worried about being made to look foolish. They had been sent a number of dried "mermaids" in the past which, in reality, were made up from the front halves of monkeys and the rear halves of large fish, cleverly stitched together. The best ones had come from China, where they had been sold to visiting sailors for high prices. Unfortunately the ship bringing the first dried platypus from Australia had stopped off in China on the way home, so it was thought that, once again, the cunning Chinese merchants had managed to fool the foreign sailors, with yet another "fantastic creature."

They did not discover their mistake for some time, but eventually the truth dawned on them. Here was a *real* animal and one to marvel at. They soon began studying it in detail. What they then discovered was that the platypus was even stranger than it appeared at first glance. Not only was its body shape very odd, but its breeding behavior was even more peculiar. It laid eggs like a bird, but then, when the babies hatched out, it suckled them with milk like a mammal.

We now know that, apart from a few spiny anteaters called echidnas, the platypus is the only mammal – out of the 4,237 different species alive today – to lay eggs. So it really is an oddity.

If that was not enough to make the experts scratch their heads, they also uncovered the fact that the male platypus carried a secret weapon, with which it injects poison into its enemies by stabbing them. Unlike a snake, which has hollow teeth to deliver its poison, the platypus uses two sharp spurs, one on the inside of each back leg, and defends itself by kicking. If it strikes a man's arm with one of these spikes, it causes agonizing pain and the arm swells up like a balloon for several days – enough to make anyone treat a platypus with great respect.

These first impressions left everyone fascinated by this new animal discovery, and the race was soon on to learn as much as possible about these remarkable creatures. Here is what they found out:

The platypus lives in burrows which it tunnels in the banks of rivers or lakes. The passageways that it digs slope upwards towards the living chamber at the far end. This means that the sleeping quarters of the platypus are above water level and are safe from flooding.

It digs in a special way. All four feet are webbed, so that the animal can swim fast under water, but the webbing on the front feet goes beyond the end of the fingers. This turns them into swimming paddles. It makes the platypus look as though it is wearing flippers, like a human swimmer. If you have ever worn flippers when snorkelling, you will know how clumsy they are on land. The platypus has the same difficulty. We humans solve the problem by taking the flippers off. The animal solves it by folding them up under its claws when it comes ashore. This leaves its powerful claws free for digging its burrow.

During the breeding season, the males and females sleep in separate beds. The male stays in the usual living quarters, but the female goes off to build her own private nesting burrow, where she will give birth and rear her young.

As the moment of egg-laying draws near, she lines her nest carefully with wet leaves. She carries these down her long tunnel, not in her hands or her mouth, but in her tail, which she curls forward to grip the leaves tight. It is important that they are moist, because she must keep her den damp. This will prevent her eggs from drying up after they have been laid.

Next she does something extraordinary. She goes to the entrance of her tunnel and starts walking down it towards the nest chamber in a special way. As she goes along the passageway, she keeps stopping. At each pause, she pushes a plug of earth into the space behind her, patting it down tight with her tail. The tunnel may be up to 36 yards in length and all along it she makes these little barriers.

Each earth-plug is about 6 inches thick and completely seals off the precious nest chamber from the outside world. Any killer, sniffing its way down the passage in search of a tasty meal will soon come across the first of these platypus earth-plugs. Suspicious, it may dig or push into it, break through and find itself once more in a tempting-looking tunnel. It sets off again, but soon comes to the second barrier. Its interest is fading now, but perhaps it is worth just one more try. So it scratches away the second plug. Then it comes to a third barrier, and that is just too much. It gives up, turns round and makes for the exit. The platypus is left undiscovered.

Safe and snug in her sealed-off nest, the female settles down to lay her eggs. There are usually only two or three of them, and they are soft to the touch. This is because, instead of having brittle shells like those of a bird, they are covered

in a rubbery skin, like reptile eggs.

These eggs are glued together in a little clump and are kept warm by the mother's big, furry body for about ten days before they are ready to hatch. During this time she does not feed. Despite her hunger she remains inside the den for days at a time, with her body curled protectively around her small brood.

On the rare occasions when she does leave the nest, she is only away for a very short time, for a quick wash and to dampen her fur. This is probably done as much to improve conditions for her eggs, as for her own benefit. She has to keep the den

humid for them and this is not an easy task. Moistening her fur once in a while can be a great help, so, when she feels the bedding in the nest is getting too dry, she sets off down the long tunnel, carefully removing the earth-plugs, one after the other. Once outside she quickly dampens her fur in some nearby water, and then without delay makes her return run down the tunnel, replacing all the earth-plugs to block it off again.

The babies, when they hatch, are tiny – not quite as long as your fingernail. Most Australian mammals keep their newborn young in a snug pouch in the fur on the underside of the mother, but the platypus does not have a pouch and cannot offer them this kind of protection. This is why it is so important to keep them inside a secure, safe nest for the first weeks of their lives.

The babies soon start to lap up the milk that is oozing from their mother's soft fur. Unlike other mammals, she has no nipples for them to suck on, so they must simply nuzzle up to her fur and lick the milk that they find seeping out of pores in her skin. It is a very primitive way of feeding the young, but then the platypus is a very primitive kind of mammal.

After about sixteen weeks the young are ready to go for their first swim and to find their own food. They set off down the tunnel, which the mother opens for them, and plunge into the water. At first they have little success in hunting, but this is not important because their mother will continue to feed them and protect them for several weeks yet.

A month later the young platypuses have finally succeeded in fending for themselves and the mother's task is over. Since her long fast in the nest, when she had to starve herself to keep the secret of her new arrivals, she has been eating greedily and has returned to her full body weight.

Few animals are such gluttons as the duck-billed platypus. To get some idea of how greedy it is, you have to imagine yourself gobbling down, in a single night, a meal weighing almost as much as you do. One captive platypus had a regular daily diet of 30 crayfish, 15.8 ounces of earthworms, 200 mealworms, 2 frogs and 2 hen's eggs.

Most animals that eat huge amounts of food do so because the things they eat are of such low food value, usually some kind of vegetation. But the platypus eats animal foods that are high in food value, making it one of the best-fed animals in the world. In the wild, all kinds of water-life are hunted, grabbed and swallowed as if the platypus will never see food again: in addition to worms, frogs and crayfish, it also takes shrimps, prawns, tadpoles, water insects and water snails – anything small that moves. Most of these are nuzzled up from the sludge on the river-bottom, and this is where its famous duckbill comes in.

This long, strange-looking nose is covered in a soft, naked, leathery skin and is full of very sensitive nerve-endings. The platypus plunges it into the mud and shoves it this way and that, until it makes contact with a suitable prey animal. Immediately, the huge snout is able to tell the hunter what it has contacted and whether it is edible. If it is, the jaws open and the object is eagerly snapped up into the mouth.

The platypus manages to do all this with both its eyes and its ears tightly shut. They are never opened under water, which means that the animal must always hunt and feed using only its senses of touch and smell.

As it is an air-breathing mammal, the platypus cannot stay under water for very long. Being rather small – only about 2 feet long – it has to come up to the surface to take a breath of air roughly once every minute. This means that each hunt has to be short and hurried.

To save time, the captured prey is usually pushed into special cheek-pouches in the platypus's mouth. With its pouches bulging, the hunter surfaces, rests a moment, and then starts crunching up its catch. Amazingly, the adult platypus has no teeth with which to do this. Instead its mouth is lined with hard, horny ridges, which it uses to crush its food. As soon as it has swallowed everything, down it goes again for another eager search in the mud.

On a typical day, the animal will hunt for only an hour in the early morning and another hour in the evening. It is not as aquatic as most people think. It can eat its fill of nutritious food and still have a great deal of time left, to rest, sleep, clean its fur and improve its burrow.

This sounds like an ideal way of life for any animal, and so it was until modern man arrived on the scene. From the platypus's point of view, the worst thing the new settlers did, apart from hunting them for their skins, was to bring rabbits with them from England. These bred in their millions and started burrowing into the river-banks, making huge warrens that drove the shy, retiring platypus away from its favorite homelands.

When people realized that the rabbits were becoming a plague in Australia and began to trap them, the platypus's troubles were far from over. There may have been fewer rabbits, but the river-bank traps set for them also easily caught and killed any of the platypuses that had managed to resist the rabbit invasion.

On top of that, fishermen started using a new kind of fish-trap in the rivers and these too caused the death of many more platypuses. When they swam into the wire-cages of the traps, they could not find their way out again. Unable to reach the surface to breathe, they soon drowned. So what had once been a very successful animal was soon in danger of becoming a rare species.

Happily, it was eventually realized that this extraordinary animal was in serious danger of disappearing and it is now completely protected. Its numbers have risen and it is thriving once more. As long as the Australian rivers do not suffer from the pollution that is spreading in so many parts of the world, the extraordinary platypus should be safe.

# The Tiger

IN THE WORLD OF ANIMALS, THE TIGER IS THE GREATEST HUNTER TO STALK the land. The largest of all the cats, bigger even than the mighty lion, it is the most powerful killer on four legs.

Its whole way of life is centered around the act of killing. As evening comes, it sets out in search of its favorite prey, usually some kind of deer. Each adult tiger lives alone and hunts alone. In the forests of Asia where it lives, it has no choice. Because of the dense vegetation, hunting in a group would not be successful.

The tiger's method of killing is to get as near to its prey as possible without being seen. This is where its wonderfully striped coat is so useful. The black stripes scattered over its orange fur make it almost invisible as it crouches, very still, in the undergrowth. The markings break up the shape of its body and camouflage it.

The tiger never creeps up on its prey from the same direction as the wind, because the breeze would carry the scent of the big cat towards its victims. Deer have a wonderful sense of smell and could quickly sniff that there was danger lurking nearby. So the stalking tiger must always approach its prey into the wind. Then the scent of the prey is blown towards the killer, helping it to check any movements, but the tiger's own smell is blown away harmlessly behind it.

After getting as close as it can by slowly creeping, pausing, crouching and then edging nearer again, the tiger finally breaks cover and makes a lightning dash straight at its prey. It has such a heavy body that it cannot sprint very far. In fact, if its final dash is over a distance of more than 100 feet, it has little hope of success.

Despite its immense power, the tiger only manages to make a kill about once in every twenty attempts. It will go hunting most evenings, and will try several times a night to bring down an animal, but because of the speed of the prey, the great cat will usually succeed no more than once a week. A tigress with young to nourish hunts harder and averages a kill about every five days.

The actual kill is quick, and the prey suffers very little. The tiger bounds forward and knocks its victim to the ground, grabbing it with both its massive front paws. The huge, curved, needle-sharp claws sink into the flesh, gripping it tight, while the tiger's jaws are clamped around its neck. Holding the prey on the ground, the tiger then squeezes its victim's throat tight and holds on until it is suffocated. Unable to breathe in the vice-like grip, the prey is soon still and lifeless.

Even after it has killed, the great tiger may stay holding on to the victim's neck for several minutes. This gives the killer time to recover from the excitement of the hunt and also makes sure that the prey really is quite dead.

Then the tiger carries its kill into the bushes and starts to eat its warm flesh. It is capable of dragging a prey animal weighing as much as 500 pounds. Sometimes a tiger has been seen to open the belly of a particularly heavy prey and remove the entrails, making it a little lighter and easier to carry.

In dense cover, hidden from the eyes of others, it gulps down an enormous meal, devouring up to 65 pounds of meat in a single night. (The equivalent of eating nearly 300 hamburgers at a single sitting.)

Quite often the tiger will refuse to leave its kill until every scrap of meat has been chewed from the bones. This may take several nights if the prey is a good-sized deer. Scavengers do not often find rich pickings at tiger kills.

If a tiger has to leave a half-eaten kill for some reason – perhaps to take a drink, or visit its cubs – it will first cover the body over with leaves, twigs and grasses. Only when it is completely hidden from the eyes of scavengers will the great hunter abandon its kill. And even then it returns as quickly as possible.

As well as deer, tigers will also kill and eat wild pigs, wild cattle, and occasionally even young rhinos or baby elephants, not to mention the domestic animals of nearby farmers.

On extremely rare occasions, a tiger has been known to kill and eat a leopard, but this usually only occurs when the slightly smaller cat has been paying too much attention to the den where a tigress's cubs are hiding.

Once in a while a tiger also turns man-eater, but this is much less common than legend would have us believe. It is normally very shy of human beings, and does its best to keep out of their way.

The tiger often has to travel for miles during a night's hunting, and its home range is huge. The area used by a single tigress can be as much as 3 miles long and 4 miles wide, which is more than the space taken up by a medium-sized town. The male tiger takes up even more space. His home range covers as much as 5 miles by 8 miles, the size of a major city.

No male tiger will ever allow another male in his territory. He shows that it belongs to him by spraying his strong-smelling urine on to special landmarks, such as tree-stumps, rocks or bushes. These personal scent signals act as a warning to any other wandering male that he is moving on to dangerous ground. After sniffing them carefully, he is likely to turn away and head off in another direction.

The tiger also marks his territory by scratching at the bark of tree-trunks and fallen logs. This produces vivid white gashes on the wood that can be seen by rivals entering his patch of forest, and special scent glands on the bottom of his feet leave behind yet another smell for his enemies to sniff.

This scent-marking makes it possible for tigers to avoid fighting one another. They are so strong that any battle between two males could hurt the winner almost as much as the loser. If the winner of the fight damaged its leg and became lame, it could not hunt for food for a time and would go hungry. So it is important, with animals as powerful as tigers, that everything must be done to avoid real violence. All their power must be kept especially for killing their prey, not for attacking one another.

Just as male tigers will not allow other males into their patch of forest, females will not permit other females to enter their space. The females also leave scent marks

and patrol the edges of their territory to make sure that no rival is trying to move in. But, although males keep out males and females keep out females, the territories of males and females do overlap a little, allowing the two sexes to meet occasionally as they prowl around their home ranges.

When they do meet, tigers have a special little greeting sound that they make. It sounds like "fuf-fuf-fuf-fuf" and shows that the animals are feeling friendly towards one another. If you make this sound when you meet a tiger in a zoo, it will look surprised for a moment and then reply with the same call. It is the tiger's way of saying "Pleased to meet you." Surprisingly, this is a signal that the lion does not use, even though it is a close relative of the tiger.

Tigers breed every two years. When the females are ready to mate, the nearby males are encouraged to visit them because of changes in the scents left on the bushes and rocks. If no males arrive, the females themselves may set off in search of mates, leaving their own home range to find them.

After a brief courtship, the male and female go their separate ways and, when the cubs are born, their father will take no part in caring for them or rearing them. It is a task for the tigress alone.

This creates a serious problem for the mother, who must leave her tiny cubs from time to time in order to hunt for food. When they are very young she often hides them in a cave or in small crevices in the rocks where they cannot be seen. When they are larger she may hide them in clumps of long grass.

It is when she is out hunting that the cubs are most likely to be killed. Large snakes, such as pythons, may sneak up on them, crush them to death and swallow them. Leopards, wild dogs and hyenas are also on the prowl, so the mother must hurry back as soon as she has managed to feed herself.

Sometimes, when the cubs are older, she returns from her kill and vomits up part of the meat she has swallowed. This soft, half-digested meat is greedily eaten by her cubs and in this way she can wean them off her milk.

Whenever she comes back to her cubs she spends some time grooming their fur, licking them with her huge, rough tongue. It is very important for them to keep their fur in good condition and, when they are tiny, they need help with this.

She also spends a great deal of time grooming her own fur, because she must make sure that any scratches or cuts she has suffered while hunting are made as clean as possible. An infection could make her go lame. A lame tiger cannot hunt, and a tiger that cannot hunt quickly starves to death. So cleanliness is vital.

Tigers are animals that seem to enjoy their creature comforts. If they overheat in the tropical jungles, they search out a small pool in which to soak themselves and cool off. As everyone knows, domestic cats hate getting wet, but tigers love it and when the daytime temperatures are very high, they will spend long spells sprawled out in the cooling waters. If the cubs are big enough the tigress will allow them to join her.

When they are half-grown, tigers are strong enough to go with their mother on the hunt. They are still too young to take part in the kill itself, but they watch eagerly from nearby cover as the tigress stalks and attacks her prey. Then, when she brings back the kill, they rush out and join her. As they look on, she opens up the body with her powerful jaws. Once the skin is pulled back and the flesh is exposed she pauses and lies down a few feet away, letting her cubs move in to feed on the fresh meat before she herself begins to eat.

The young tigers can easily follow their mother's movements in the undergrowth because she has some bright markings on the backs of her ears. On each ear there is a large white spot surrounded by a black edge. From a distance this looks like a pair of big eyes and the cubs can see this very clearly, even if the rest of their mother's body is hidden in the long grass. Because the markings are on the backs of the ears, they are not visible to the prey the tigress is stalking. These same markings are used when two tigers are threatening one another. When they become angry they turn their ears round so that the backs face forwards, displaying the "eye-spots" to the opponent. This acts as a warning signal.

The final stage of rearing the young tigers comes when they are about two years old. It is a strange, quiet moment without any fuss. One day the tigress simply gets up and walks away from her cubs and leaves them on their own. She does not look back and never returns. Then, for the first time, the young animals will have to fend for themselves, and make all their own kills, if they are to survive in the jungle.

Many of the cubs die when they are very young. From each litter of two or three cubs, usually only one will manage to grow to full adulthood. The others will become prey themselves before they are big enough to frighten away all the killers that try to attack them.

Those that do manage to grow into fully adult tigers have little to fear from the other animals in the jungle. Only human hunters can offer them any serious threat. Unfortunately, during the past few centuries, more and more men with weapons have invaded the forests and destroyed as many tigers as they could find.

Some men did it to protect their farm animals; some did it to collect the beautiful tiger-skins as trophies; some did it to show how brave they were; and some did it simply for sport. Today we despise such men, but in the past they often boasted loudly of their hunting victories. One Maharajah announced: "My total bag of tigers is one thousand one hundred and fifty only."

It is little wonder that the magnificent tiger has become a rare species and that there are only about 4,000 of them left in the wild. Their numbers were even smaller than this some years ago, but there are now special tiger reserves set aside for them, where hunting is not permitted and where farmers are not allowed to settle. There are plenty of wild deer and other prey animals living in these reserves, so that the big cats do not go hungry. They may not have the vast spaces to roam which they once enjoyed, but at least they appear to be safe now from complete destruction.

# The Beaver

AT FIRST SIGHT, THE BEAVER LOOKS LIKE A GIANT RAT WITH A FLAT TAIL. When you meet one it does not seem very exciting. With its dull brown color and its wet, bedraggled fur it is hardly one of nature's beauties. If we saw the animal sitting in a zoo cage we could be forgiven for ignoring it. But this would be a terrible mistake, because the beaver is one of the most extraordinary animals alive. This is not because of what it *is*, but because of what it *does*.

The beaver is the master-builder of the animal world. It is not exaggerating to say that it has changed whole landscapes. It is also true that, apart from man, it has fashioned the largest buildings ever seen on this planet. One of them was nearly half a mile long.

It fells trees, builds dams, clears canals, constructs houses and stocks larders. Its dams have created lakes, prevented floods and altered vegetation. It is one of the busiest animals on earth and also, because of its fine fur, one of the most hunted.

What is it that makes the beaver such a hard worker? Why does it not relax and enjoy the lovely spring weather, or the warm summer sun? Why does it never stop "beavering about"?

The answer is that it lives in the cold rivers and lakes of the northern lands, where to survive through the winter is not easy. Some animals simply burrow deep into the ground and go fast asleep until the warm weather returns. The beaver does not do this. Instead it defeats the bad weather by making a snug den for itself with a well-stocked larder nearby.

This is not as simple as it sounds, because the water levels keep changing. The beaver's house, or lodge, must not be flooded, nor must it be left high and dry. To understand the way the animal deals with this problem, it helps to start at the beginning, as a young beaver leaves the family home and strikes out on its own.

When it is two years old, the beaver's childhood is over and it leaves its parents for good. It may swim many miles away, looking for the ideal spot it can call its own. Once there, it digs a burrow in the mud of the river-bank. The entrance hole is under the water and, as it digs, the animal makes the tunnel slope up higher and higher. Once the passageway has risen above the water level of the river, the animal widens the tunnel out into a den.

The beaver can feed, sleep and, later on, breed inside this space, but the den needs a great deal of cleaning and repair. For instance, if the water in the river rises higher, the den will soon become flooded. The beaver deals with this crisis by scraping mud from the roof of the den. This mud falls to the floor, the floor rises up and the flooding is cured.

This is a simple way of avoiding a flood in the den, but if the water continues to rise, the problem quickly returns. The beaver goes back to scraping away the ceiling

and letting it fall on the floor again. This may happen several times, but one day the den rises so high that its ceiling breaks through the surface of the earth on the river-bank. Now the den has an open top and the beaver is easy prey for any passing hunter. The answer to this is to build a new roof, a huge thick one that even a bear will find hard to get through when searching for a meal.

This new roof is made of sticks, branches, stones and mud. From a distance it looks like a circular pyramid. Inside it, the beaver's snug den is safe from the winter weather – the freezing rain, the snow storms and the howling winds. No matter how high the water level rises, the hard-working beaver can match it by increasing the height of the den inside the "lodge."

In some cases the water floods so much that it completely surrounds the lodge. The pile of sticks and stones now looks as though it has been built in the middle of a pond, instead of on the bank of a river. This helps even more to protect it from wandering killers.

A completely different problem has to be faced if, instead of rising, the water level falls. If this happens, the entrance to the beaver's tunnel can be seen on the dried-up river-bank. Instead of being carefully hidden beneath the water, it is on view to any hungry animal prowling near the river. It is also exposed to the freezing winter blizzards. So somehow the water level must not be allowed to fall below the entrance. It is a matter of life and death.

The beaver's way of solving this problem is amazing. It sets about building a huge dam. This barrier slows down the flow of the water in the river. As it slows and its level rises, the river spreads out sideways, sometimes creating a small lake. By carefully adjusting the dam the beavers can keep the level of the water just where they want it – not too high and not too low. When the rains come, the dam can be opened up a little. When the drought comes, the dam can be closed up tighter.

To build the dam, the beaver has to cut down trees and drag them into place. This is exhausting work, but the beaver has wonderful teeth with which to carry it out. Its front teeth are long and shaped like chisels. Unlike human teeth, they never stop growing. As they are worn down by the endless gnawing, they re-grow, so that they are always the right length for the task.

The beaver selects a tree not far from the river-bank, usually a small one with a trunk that is only about 3 to 8 inches across, and begins biting at it. The animal's tongue is folded back into its throat, completely blocking it off and preventing any wood-chips from disappearing down its gullet. It gnaws away at the tree-trunk, moving round it as it does so.

It takes about five minutes to cut through a 3-inch tree. Then there is a creaking sound that means the tree is about to topple over. As soon as it hears this sound, the beaver makes a wild dash to get out of the way before the tree crashes to the ground. Sometimes it is too slow and is squashed flat by the tree, but this is very rare. It nearly always seems to know which way the trunk is going to fall.

Once it has felled the tree, the beaver starts to cut it up into sections. The thicker the tree, the shorter these sections are. These "logs" are then carried or dragged away towards the site of the dam. Small branches are carried in the teeth. Heavier branches are pulled into the water and floated along. Very heavy tree-trunks – those more than 4 inches – are left where they fall and only their small side-branches are used.

On land the beaver sometimes carries small objects in a strange way. It rears up and plods along on its hind legs. While it does this it holds its load in its front feet and its mouth. (It also, incidentally, uses this same upright posture when carrying its young.)

Once it arrives at the dam with its prize, the beaver pushes and shoves, pulls and tugs, until it has managed to ram the new branch into the mass already there. Mud and stones are added and soon the dam begins to look like a great wall. Some dams are so strong that men have been able to cross rivers by riding over them on horseback. One was over 2,000 feet from end to end.

In some places, big dams have been used over and over again, as the seasons have come and gone. When old beavers died, new beavers came and added a little more to the dams. In one case a dam was found to be a thousand years old. It was like the beaver's version of the Great Wall of China.

As well as its house and its dam, the beaver also builds long canals. It does this

by digging in marshy places with its front feet, loosening the mud and pushing it to one side or the other. The canals are made in the summer months and are used by the animals to swim from one feeding area to another, or for moving building logs through the water.

Summer feeding is easy. There is plenty of lush vegetation and the beavers gorge themselves on fresh grasses, leaves and stems. When winter comes it is another matter. In the bleak northern landscape everything freezes. Above ground there is nothing to eat. Even the rivers freeze over with a thick layer of solid ice.

How do the beavers survive these terrible winter months? The answer is that they build an underwater larder. They make this special food store at the end of the summer. As the days shorten and the cold winds start to blow, they collect fresh young stems and small branches, carry them in their teeth down to the river-bed near their home and push them into the soft mud there. Time after time they make these trips, until they have a big enough supply to see them through the frozen days ahead.

Just before winter comes, they add a thick layer of mud all over the top of their house. This freezes solid and keeps out hungry killers that might be prowling about outside. Then the beaver family goes below, enters its den and crowds together for warmth. After the rivers have frozen over, they can swim along beneath the ice to the nearby larder, pull out a stick or stem that has been kept refrigerator-fresh in the icy cold water, and carry it back to the den. There they can enjoy their meals in peace, while the weather rages outside.

If they are running short of air beneath the ice they can solve that problem, too. They swim to their nearby dam and cut holes in it with their teeth. This makes the water flow through faster and the level of the unfrozen water sinks a little, leaving an air space between the water and the underside of the ice. This means that the beavers can, if they wish, swim on the surface of the water when collecting stems from their food stores. It is rather as though they have built themselves a large indoor swimming pool, with a roof of ice above their heads.

So the secret of their success, and the reason for all their hard work, is that they can spend the whole of the winter under the ice in safety. Each beaver lodge contains an entire family, living together. There is the adult pair, their older "kits" (as young beavers are called) and their younger ones. The pair mate for life and have only one litter of kits each year. So a beaver family usually consists of a dozen or so animals at any one time. All but the youngest ones help with the building work.

They share other duties, too. When a new litter is born in the spring everyone brings them food, with the father supplying more than anyone else. They are peaceful families, with hardly any fighting or squabbling. The mother and father are excellent parents, protecting their young and rearing them with great care. Whenever there is any sign of danger, they give a special beaver alarm signal. This is a violent slap of their heavy, flat tails on the surface of the water. It makes a loud noise that can be heard all over their territory and warns the younger ones that they must take cover.

It is tempting to think that, like humans, beavers learn all their "skills" from their parents and pass them on, in turn, to their children. They give the impression of being incredibly intelligent animals. It is certainly true that they are very bright, but much of what they do comes automatically to them and does not have to be learned.

As an experiment, young beavers, born in a zoo, were taken away from their parents and placed in a new zoo-paddock containing a stream. They had never seen a beaver pond in their lives before, but immediately set about building a lodge and a dam. They did this without making mistakes or having any second thoughts, proving that their building actions are inborn and not learned.

The beaver is clearly a remarkable animal and it is now well protected in the wild. This was not always the case. When human hunters first came to explore the far north, they found it an easy prey. The animals were killed in their millions for their fur. Both the North American and the European beavers were nearly wiped out, but eventually hunting was banned and the few remaining survivors were left alone.

These lucky ones soon started breeding in large numbers and began spreading out once more into their old homelands. Eventually they were so successful, and there were so many of them, that the hunters were allowed to return.

This time, though, the hunting has been carefully controlled and only a limited number of beavers can be killed each year for the fur trade. Their future is secure at last. All over the northern lands, their dams can now be seen again and their amazing building feats are once more changing the shape of the riverside landscape.

# The Rhino

RHINOS HAVE BEEN ROAMING THE PLAINS OF TROPICAL AFRICA FOR 40 MILLION years. For ages they had little to fear and lived quiet, untroubled lives. They altered hardly at all. They were so successful there was no need to change.

Their huge bodies made it impossible for the smaller killers to attack them. Their leather-tough, nearly one-inch-thick skin made it difficult for even the biggest killers to bite them. And the massive horns sticking out at the front of their heads made it dangerous for even the most desperate killers to approach them.

They were lords of the land in which they lived. They had become so massive, so physically powerful and so fearless that nothing could touch them. It seemed like the perfect solution, the safest way of life in the world. They even had a trick for dealing with the tiny skin-pests that plague so many other large tropical animals. They allowed small birds to sit on their backs, scamper around their bodies and peck away these pests. It gave the birds a good meal and it kept their skins clean. The fact that rhinos are naked, without the usual coat of hair, made it easy for their tick-birds to carry out their duties.

Then, into this perfect world came a new threat, against which they had no answer. Primitive human hunters arrived on the scene and began killing the rhinos – trapping and spearing them for their meat. At first this was not too serious. There were, as yet, very few people and there were hundreds of thousands of rhinos. They were hard to kill and there were many other kinds of prey to choose from, so our early ancestors did not cause them too much trouble.

As the years passed, however, human weapons improved. Human cunning outwitted the lumbering power of the great animals. And when guns arrived on the scene, the problem became serious. Other animals ran away when the guns started blazing, but the fearless rhinos simply turned and charged at their killers. In doing so they made themselves easier targets, and fell in their thousands.

The first big-game hunters were brave men with badly made guns. They took terrible risks as they set off on safaris, trekking into the unknown realms of the "Dark Continent." They knew little or nothing about the way of life of the animals they encountered and needed great courage to face these "wild beasts" on foot in what was to them strange, mysterious country. They proudly brought home their trophies to hang on their walls and impress their friends.

Later these men were followed by a new breed of hunter, this time with high-powered rifles with telescopic sights. They set off in the safety of trucks and jeeps and had little to fear. They knew the country now, had expert guides and maps, understood the animals and no longer needed courage. They lined up the rhinos in their sights and gunned them down in complete safety. It was about as brave as shooting a cow in a field.

These new big-game hunters were cowards pretending to be heroes. When they returned home they told terrible tales of rhinos charging their trucks and denting them with their horns. What they failed to mention was that they had deliberately taunted the animals by driving right into the middle of their special home-patches and had even chased them to make them angry. If they had approached quietly and with respect, the rhinos would have left them in peace, as something not worth bothering about. But any rhino that feels threatened will obviously react by defending itself.

So the stories about violent, bad-tempered animals spread and spread. Everyone believed them and the rhino was labelled as a brutal trouble-maker, when in reality it was these cowardly, well-protected new hunters who were causing all the violence. We now know that the rhino, far from being stupid and savage, is in fact highly intelligent, sensitive and peaceful. Its bad reputation was a lie created by big-game hunters. Rhinos were only aggressive if driven to take measures to defend themselves.

Recently it has been discovered that if rhinos are treated kindly they can become delightfully tame and can even be taken for a walk like a pet dog. One rhino expert, who had saved a baby rhino and reared it until it was adult, found that despite its great size the animal still insisted on coming inside her house. One day it tried to push through into her dining-room and became firmly stuck in the doorway. She only managed to free it by pouring lots of oil over its body, so that its rough skin became slippery, and it could slide back out again. After that she built a stockade around her house to stop her far too friendly rhino from entering and getting jammed again.

Despite our growing understanding about the true nature of these fascinating animals, their numbers sank lower and lower. As farming became more popular in tropical Africa, more space was needed for the growing human population. This gave further excuses for killing off large numbers of rhinos. One man alone, employed to clear land of dangerous animals for a new farming project, slaughtered a thousand rhinos in only two years. That was just one example, and it was repeated almost everywhere.

Eventually, there were hardly any rhinos left in Africa and the killing had to stop. The rhino was made a protected animal. It could return to its quiet way of life once more and start breeding again. That at least was the idea, but now a new threat came. Poachers began to take over where the big-game hunters had left off.

These poachers were not after the rhino meat. They did not want to put stuffed rhino heads on their walls as trophies. All they wanted were the horns. They could get huge prices for rhino horn and they went about their work in a brutally business-like way. Instead of rifles, they used sub-machine guns. Attacking at night, they moved swiftly. Rhinos are heavy sleepers and are easily surprised after dark. The poachers drove up, sprayed the sleepy rhinos with bullets, leapt out of their trucks armed with chain-saws, quickly cut off the precious horns, and sped away leaving the dead bodies for the vultures.

Time after time they struck until almost all the rhinos were gone. Now, instead

of the hundreds of thousands that used to roam the plains of Africa, there are just a few left, often with armed guards patrolling nearby to protect them from the next night-raid of the poachers. Despite all the help these survivors are getting from game wardens and other devoted helpers, their future is far from safe.

Why is the rhino horn so valuable? It is made of tightly packed hair, formed into a hard spike, and has no medicinal value. Despite this, in some parts of India it is ground down into a powder and used as a love-potion. In certain regions of the Middle East no man can claim to be important unless he has a dagger with a rhino-horn handle. Without it he would be a "nobody." In China many years ago it was believed that a cup or a bowl made out of rhino horn would make a drink fizz if it contained poison. To own such a cup or bowl was seen as a matter of life and death at a time when poisoning was commonplace. Even today, the horn is still in demand in China for making a powder that is used to treat various illnesses. In Taiwan, rhino horns are employed as a kind of money.

In all these cases, people will pay huge sums for a large, new rhino horn. A single horn can be worth as much as a year's wages to an African and it is not hard to see why some men are prepared to risk jail to steal one.

Because it is only the horn that the poachers want, someone had the bright idea of catching all the rhinos without hurting them, carefully removing their horns and letting them go again. Then the animals could live in peace once more without fear of attack because to the horn-hunters they would be worthless.

This is a good idea and before long it may have to be done, but it is sad to think of these magnificent animals wandering around without their famous weapons. The rhinos themselves might find it a difficult solution, too, because they use their horns in a surprising number of ways.

We think of the horns as being employed only in defence, when rhinos are charging their enemies, but that is a mistake. They also use them when fighting rivals during the breeding season, sparring with each other like swordsmen. They use them again during courtship, when they make a special "dust-sweeping" display. They hook down branches, turn over logs and strip the bark from dead trees with them when feeding, especially when there is a drought. They dig up bulbs and roots with them. They also use them to dig for salt and, above all, for water in dried-up river-beds. In moments of emotion, the horn is used to caress a companion or to punish one. Finally, mother rhinos employ them to steer their young, nudging them along in the right direction as they move from place to place.

So, if rhinos do have to be de-horned, they will often find themselves in difficulty. Their worst problem will come at times of drought. Then, they may need special help to dig for water or obtain extra food. De-horning is not a step that can be taken lightly, but one day it may be the only way to save these animals from becoming extinct.

What are the chances for rhinos in the future? How many remain alive in the world today? In addition to the African rhinos, there are still a few left in parts of Asia. Altogether today there are five different kinds still struggling to survive.

First, there is the African black rhinoceros, the one pictured here. It used to be possible to say that this was the "common" rhino, but now the best we can say is that it is one of the "least rare." Thirty years ago a careful count was done and it was discovered that their numbers had dropped to 13,500. Although this was a small figure compared with the hundreds of thousands that had been present a hundred years earlier, it was still enough to make us feel that this kind of rhino was safe for the future. Sadly we were wrong. The poachers became more and more violent and now there are only 3,700 black rhinos left.

Second, there is the African white rhinoceros, which is the largest of all. In fact, apart from the elephants, it is the biggest of all living land mammals. It weighs over 8,800 pounds and is 13.8 feet long, compared with a mere 4,400 pounds and 10.8 feet for its black relative. Again, there are only a few thousand left.

Despite their names, the black and white rhinos are both grey in color. The real difference, apart from size, is in the shape of their mouths. The black rhino has a pointed upper lip, used to pluck leaves when the animal is browsing from low bushes. The white rhino has a blunt, wide mouth, that is more useful when it is grazing in the long grass.

Third, there is the Sumatran rhinoceros, the smallest of all. It weighs only 2,200 pounds and is no more than 8 feet long. Unlike the other four kinds of rhino it is covered with straggly hair and is sometimes called "the hairy rhino." Apart from Sumatra, there are thought to be a few left in the hill forests of Myanmar (Burma), peninsular Malaysia and the island of Borneo. It is very rare indeed and, at the last count, there were no more than 150 left in the entire world. Like the African rhinos, the little Sumatran has two horns and, again like them, has been hunted for these for many years. The hunters have now nearly exhausted their supply.

Fourth, there is the Javan rhinoceros, the rarest of all. There are only about 50 left, all kept in one small game reserve in western Java. This rhino has also been hunted for its horns, although it has little to offer in that respect. It is a small animal, again only weighing about 2,200 pounds. The male has only a single horn and the female no horn at all, so hunters can never have enjoyed big prizes. Despite this, the Javan rhino has been destroyed everywhere in its wild habitat and can now only survive under complete protection from game wardens.

Fifth, there is the Indian rhinoceros, the most heavily armored of all, with its thick skin thrown into heavy folds, looking like armour plating. It is very similar to the Javan, except that it is bigger – at 4,400 pounds – and the female has a horn as well as the male. Like the Javan, it no longer survives in the wild and is found only in protected game reserves. There are about 1,500 of them left in eight separate reserves in Nepal, Bengal and Assam. Its horns are not very impressive, and it prefers to defend itself by slashing with its sharp, tusk-like teeth. Despite this, poachers still try to sneak into the reserves in search of horns to make (quite useless) love-potions.

Those, then, are the five kinds of rhino surviving today. Even added together, there are only a few thousand of them and yet they are still being tracked down and killed. In the past, feeling superior, we have called them stupid beasts, but perhaps after we have lost them forever we will realize that it is not the rhinos, but we who are the stupid ones.

# The Bush Baby

MANY PEOPLE THINK THAT THE BUSH BABY GETS ITS NAME BECAUSE IT has a bushy tail and because it has a soft, rounded body, big eyes and a flat face like a human baby. But the truth is that the animal was given its name, not because of its bushy coat, but because it lives in the African bush, and not because it looks like a baby, but because it cries like one.

Bush babies are night animals, sleeping during the day in a nest of leaves or in a hollow tree and coming out to search for food as dusk falls. In the growing darkness they call to one another with a high-pitched cry that sounds like a human baby in distress.

Although bush babies are related to the monkeys and apes, the first time you see one scampering about in the bushes it reminds you more of a squirrel than a monkey. It is an amazing jumper and can make huge leaps from one tree to another, landing with the skill of a circus acrobat. It can even change direction in mid-air by using its long, bushy tail as a rudder. Its back legs are much longer than its front ones and it starts a leap by bending these and then pushing them out straight as it takes off. In the air, all four of its limbs are stretched out fully, ready to grab hold of the branch at which it has aimed itself, and to cushion the shock of landing.

The speed with which these little animals can fling themselves around in the trees at night has to be seen to be believed. They are so fast that nothing could possibly catch them. In fact, in the dim light it is almost impossible to follow them with your eyes. Their secret is that their own eyes are much better in poor light than ours. With their huge black pupils fully opened, they can see as clearly in the dusk as we can at midday.

As they leap about at the start of an evening's hunting, they disturb the insects that have just settled down to pass the night clinging to a twig or a leaf. As soon as these insects begin to move about, the bush baby's alert eyes spot them and, with a quick dart, they are caught. They are always grabbed in a special way. The bush baby clings on to a branch with its hind feet and flings its body forward. At the same moment it snatches out with its hands and takes hold of the prey with its fingers. It then quickly moves it up to its mouth, where it starts to munch on it with its small, needle-sharp teeth.

The bush baby is so fast and so accurate when it is hunting that it is even capable of snatching a tiny gnat that is flying in the air nearby. In taking its prey, its big eyes are helped by its sensitive ears. These are wonderfully mobile and seem to be forever twitching and twisting this way and that, as the animal moves around in the branches. On the insides of the ears you can just see little rib-like folds of skin. These help to direct into the ears the sounds of even the quietest, most minute insect imaginable. In fact, the bush baby is rather like a bat that cannot fly, and can use the same echo-location that bats employ when hunting insects at night.

With this echo-location system the animal sends out a stream of very high-pitched squeaks. If these tiny sounds – so high that we humans cannot hear them – hit an object they bounce back and the echo reaches the ears of the hunter. The closer an object is the quicker the sound comes back. Also, if the object is moving, the echoes change, giving clues about its position, speed and direction. Against a detection weapon like this, no insect is safe, even at night.

In addition to insects, bush babies also eat small mice, lizards, tree-frogs, young birds, eggs, snails, fruits and berries. When they have finished feeding they clean themselves very carefully, grooming their fur with their lower teeth. These teeth are narrow and each one is like the "tooth" of a little comb. When their dense fur has been well combed, their toilet is nearly done, but they still have to put a finishing touch to it. This consists of a satisfying scratch around the back of the neck – the one place their tooth-comb cannot reach. They even have a special claw to carry out this scratching. All their fingers and toes have flat nails, rather like ours, except for the second toe. This toe, on each hind foot, has a sharp claw instead of a blunt nail and is used as the "scratching claw." It is also employed to clean out the all-important ears, which have to be kept in perfect condition.

As if good vision and good hearing were not enough, the bush babies also have a very keen sense of smell. Unlike their monkey relatives, they have a moist nose. In this respect they are more like dogs than monkeys and, also like dogs, they can detect their prey by scent with great accuracy.

They can also use their noses to trace their own movements and those of their companions. They do this in an extraordinary way. Every so often they pause and raise one foot off the branch. They spray a few drops of their urine on to the sole of the foot and rub it against one of their hands. Then they raise the other foot and repeat the action. Now both their palms and both the soles of their feet are smeared with their scented urine and, as they clamber about on the branches, they automatically leave a personal scent trail wherever they go.

Given their wonderful sense organs, the bush babies find it easy enough to obtain their food. They are very successful animals, found all over tropical Africa in a wide variety of places ranging from humid rainforests to dry bushlands. Because they sleep by day, visitors to the game-parks do not see much of them and often fail to realize just how common they are.

The females all have small, fixed areas where they live and they never stray from these. The males have bigger territories and a boss male will travel around visiting one female after another, checking to see if any of them are ready to mate.

The baby is born in a nest of twigs and leaves. When it is very young it is not carried around on the mother's body like a baby monkey. She leaves it in the nest while she goes hunting, but on these occasions is never away for very long. When it is a little older, she takes it with her when she moves about, and she is more likely to carry it by the scruff of the neck, like a cat, than let it cling to her fur.

The young are weaned when they are about three months old. At this stage they

are able to follow the mother around actively at night when she goes hunting. She allows them to stay near her until they are grown up, towards the end of their second year. If they are females, they may stay on in their mother's territory even when they are adults. As a result of this, it is not uncommon to see a group of related females and their babies living together in a small group. The young males, however, must leave the maternal home and fend for themselves elsewhere.

Bush babies have few enemies, but they are wary and are always on the lookout for possible trouble. If they have to go down on to the ground, when moving from one clump of bushes to another, they are particularly uneasy and, instead of running along on the ground, dash across the open space like miniature kangaroos, hopping along on their hind legs as quickly as possible.

Like many animals, they have a special body coloring that helps to make them less easy to see. Their brown fur is paler on the underside of their bodies. This kind of shading is called counter-shading because it works counter to the shading caused by the light of the sun or the moon. When the light falls on the animal from the sky above, the animal's tummy is in shadow. So, if its fur was the same color all over, its underside would appear darker. Its back, being more brightly lit, would appear paler. But because the belly-fur on the bush baby is lighter than its back-fur, its special coloring counter-acts this. The result is that the animal appears flat and does not show up so clearly as it sits on a branch. This helps to hide it from the eyes of hungry killers.

You may well wonder how a bush baby is ever caught for a zoo. If it is so amazingly acrobatic, is so well hidden by its counter-shaded brown fur, and only comes out at night, how on earth do collectors manage to capture one? The answer is that bush babies do have one terrible weakness. They love drinking wine. The collectors simply put out some palm wine, wait until the bush babies are drunk and sleepy and then pick them up without any trouble at all.

# The Bear

WE ARE ALL FAMILIAR WITH THE FRIENDLY "TEDDY BEAR," BUT WHAT WOULD happen if we met a real bear? Would it be so friendly? What are the true facts about the wild, brown bear?

When they are born, baby bears are anything but cuddly. They are tiny, naked and blind and look more like fat rats than baby bears. There are usually two born in a litter, and even if you put the two of them together on the scales they would weigh less than the book you are holding. The mother bear is at least a hundred times heavier than her cubs.

The cubs are born in a snug, underground den. The den is prepared by the mother at the start of the long, cold winter. If she cannot find a quiet corner in a cave, she digs in the earth beneath some rocks or an old tree, and makes a hole big enough to hold both her and her babies. Then she curls up and goes to sleep.

Two or three months later, the babies are born. Outside the den it is the dead of winter and freezing cold, but the tiny cubs are kept warm by the huge body of their mother. They stay inside the den with her for another three or four months, feeding on her milk. Then, with the arrival of spring weather, the cubs step out into the sunlight for the first time.

It is at this stage that they really do look like toy teddy bears. Small, rounded, furry and with a bouncy playfulness, they start to explore the exciting world outside the den. Their mother stays close by, watching them carefully, and defending them against any enemies that try to attack. Because of the immense strength of the mother bear, the cubs have little to fear from anything except human hunters.

They follow their mother around as she goes off in search of food. She eats many different things, but always seeks out the juiciest food she can find. She uses her wonderful sense of smell to track down ripe fruits, berries and nuts. She digs in the ground with her powerful claws for roots and bulbs. She hunts for frogs in small ponds, and catches salmon in the fast-moving rivers. If she discovers the nest of a breeding bird, she gobbles up a quick meal of raw eggs. If she finds the tunnels of burrowing rats or mice, she sniffs the ground with her huge nose and then starts scrabbling in the earth with her paws, digging down to the hidden nests below. If her prey are too slow, or are trapped in the falling earth, she snaps them up greedily in her powerful jaws.

If she spots larger prey animals, she charges at them with a galloping run that is amazingly fast for such a heavily built animal. It is claimed that she can reach speeds as high as 30 miles an hour. Catching up with a small deer, she kills it with strong blows from her front feet. Unfortunately, she also kills domestic sheep if she gets the chance, and this makes her the enemy of local farmers. As a result, bears have been hunted down and killed in their thousands every year since farming first began.

If nothing else is available, bears will eat dead animals and even insects. And, yes, bears really do like honey and they are prepared to put up with hundreds of stings from angry bees to get it.

The young bears grow fast throughout the summer and, feeding alongside their mother, learn the best things to eat and those to avoid. When winter comes they return together to their sleeping den. This time, the mother does not produce any new babies in the den. She slumbers, curled up snugly, with her older cubs.

When the next spring arrives they will all set off feeding again, but this time the much bigger cubs will probably go off on their own and by the time their third winter arrives they will make their own dens. When they have left, the mother mates again with a wandering male and is ready once more to produce another litter when she takes to her winter den.

Each female bear lives on a particular patch of land – her feeding ground. The male bear is less territorial. He wanders about, covering a much greater area and passing through the territories of several females. He is always ready to mate with one in the summer, if she is prepared to start a new family. And the female will mate with any male who comes her way.

The males are much bigger and more powerful than the females, but they do not use their great strength to defend their mates. In fact, they have very little time for them. Once a male has mated, he leaves it to the female to carry out all the parental duties. She must rear the cubs entirely on her own. His enormous size and power are needed as a defence against rival male bears. These males will try to frighten him away from the females, so that they can mate with them instead. Each male must look as huge as possible if it is to scare its rivals away.

Wild bears sometimes attack humans who visit the forests where they live. These attacks are really a mistake. Although bears have a wonderful sense of smell, their eyesight is not so good. If they see a human being walking along they think it might be a rival bear rearing itself up on to its hind legs in a threat display. So they charge, rear up and threaten back. If the human happens to be a deer-hunter with a gun, he often panics and shoots the bear. If he is unarmed he is sometimes killed by the bear, and the fact that he is hardly ever eaten after he has been killed confirms that the bear was seeing him, not as a prey animal, but as a rival.

Brown bears need so much living space that their numbers have fallen lower and lower. In Britain, the last bears were killed a thousand years ago. In France today there are only 30 left alive in the wild. In the whole of Europe only 300 remain. They are doing better in the colder regions of North America, Scandinavia and Russia, but even there the hunters are killing many of them each year.

The brown bear is only one of seven different kinds that exist today. It is the most widespread and the most common. The brown bears that come from Kodiak Island in the far north are the heaviest of all land meat-eaters. A big male may measure up to 9 feet in height when it rears itself up, dwarfing the human figure. The well-known grizzly bear is another large variety of brown bear found in the colder regions of North America.

A much smaller, quieter animal is the American black bear. This has also been hunted down and shot, year after year, by so-called sportsmen, but it manages to survive because of its intelligence and its shy personality.

In South America there is only one kind, the rare spectacled bear. It has rings of white fur around its eyes, as though it is wearing huge sunglasses. Today there are only 2,000 of them left in the world. They like the damp, hot forests where they climb the trees in search of fruits. If they have eaten well, they make themselves a bed of broken branches, high up in trees, and take a snooze there before continuing with their search for food.

There are three other tropical bears, all living in the hot forests of Asia. They are the shaggy sloth bear, the small sun bear and the stocky Asian black bear. All have coats of black fur with pale markings on their chests.

The sloth bear has a very big snout and long curved claws. It uses its powerful feet to dig into termite hills or to tear away the bark of trees in its search for insect food. It can close its nostrils completely and, when it has found its prey, it pushes its long nose into the hole it has made and sucks the insects into its tube-like mouth.

The sun bear is the smallest of all. Its body is little more than 3 feet long. Shy animals, not dangerous to man, they are night-time feeders. They are the most agile climbers. In fact, they spend most of their time aloft in the trees, resting there during the day on small platforms of twigs and branches.

The Asian black bear, sometimes called the moon bear because of the pale moon-shaped patch on its chest, is a big-eared animal with a broad mane of hair around its neck and shoulders. It is twice as heavy as the little sun bear, but its way of life in the trees of the tropical forests of Asia is much the same.

Finally, there is the beautiful white polar bear with its huge, streamlined body, its massive feet and its very long neck. Unlike all the other bears, the polar bear eats only meat. It is a ferocious killer that prefers to attack and eat seals whenever it can find them. Groups of polar bears also gather around the bodies of dead whales that have been washed ashore, to feast on their flesh.

Although it is not as heavy as the biggest of the brown bears, the polar bear can claim to be the longest bear, the males reaching 6 feet from nose to tail. They are great travellers. In their endless search for food in the frozen wastes of the far north, they may travel more than 600 miles in a year and may cover many miles in a single day. Imagine what it must be like for such an animal to be shut up in a small zoo cage for the whole of its life.

All the bears are magnificent animals and yet they have nearly always been badly treated by humans. If we gave as much affection to real bears as we do to our toy teddy bears, they would have a much better chance of surviving. If we continue to hunt them and kill them as ruthlessly as we have in the past, they will soon vanish forever.

Most of us owned a toy teddy when we were very young, but few know how it got its name. Why a Teddy Bear? Why not a Freddie Bear or a Billy Bear? Many people think that Teddy is short for Edward, but that is not the case.

The true story is as follows: Ninety years ago the President of the United States was on a bear hunt in Mississippi. His hosts were very upset because they could not find a big bear for him to shoot. As a last resort they brought him a little bear cub, so that his visit would not be a complete failure. Seeing the sad little animal, the President refused to kill it. A cartoon appeared in a newspaper showing this event and praising him for his kindness to the cub. The little bear became famous overnight.

The President's name was Theodore Roosevelt and his nickname was Teddy, which is short for Theodore. The bear became known as "Teddy's Bear" and soon appeared as a popular toy. After a while "Teddy's Bear" became shortened to "Teddy Bear." That all happened back in 1902 and ever since teddys have continued to be comforting friends for millions of children.

# The Dolphin

EVERYONE LOVES DOLPHINS. THEY SEEM TO BE THE PERFECT EXAMPLE of animal friendliness, energy and good humor. Television programs and films have taken us down into their underwater world more and more often, until we feel they have become old friends. They have sometimes been said to have almost magical powers, but what are they really like?

The dolphin is a whale in miniature. Its smooth-skinned, hairless body is beautifully streamlined and wonderfully athletic. With beats from its powerful flippers and with strong up-and-down thrusts from its muscular tail, it can reach speeds of over 20 miles an hour.

Because it is only about the size of a seal, with little weight to carry, it can leap high out of the water, curving in a great arc before plunging back into the waves again. Anyone who has been close to a group of wild dolphins in the ocean as they jump, dive and weave this way and that, will never forget the sight. It is a delight to be able to watch an animal that is so wonderfully in tune with its watery world.

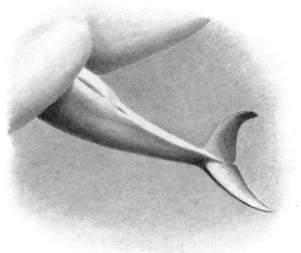

The dolphin starts out life as a 3-foot-long baby, looking just like a small version of its mother. Being a mammal that lives its entire life in the sea, its first problem, as soon as it is born, is how to get a breath of air. Having no gills, it cannot breathe under water like a fish. After it slides, tail-first, from its mother's body, it may manage to struggle up to the surface on its own, but if it is too weak it will need assistance. Luckily help is always close at hand because, whenever a baby is due to be born, the mother's female companions act like midwives. They cluster around and stay ready to raise the newborn dolphin up to the surface. They also keep an eye open for any possible dangers and protect both the mother and her baby from approaching enemies.

The baby will stay with its mother, feeding on her milk like any other mammal, for several years. This is a very long time for a baby to be suckled by its mother, but there is a lot to learn in the world of dolphins and childhood must not be rushed.

Every so often the mother needs to set off for some high-speed fish-hunting and to do this she must leave her baby behind. She cannot simply abandon it on its own, and once again she is given assistance by her female companions. While she is away, one of them acts as a babysitter, caring for and protecting her baby until she returns. As soon as she reappears, she is greeted by excited squeaks from her infant.

This helpfulness is typical of the dolphin's whole way of life. They not only act as midwives and babysitters for young dolphins, they also care for adults that are sick or injured. The companions of the animal in trouble push their heads under its flippers and gently raise it to the surface. They hold it up there so that it can take in air through its blowhole. If they did not do this it would soon drown.

So strong is the dolphin's urge to help a drowning animal that it has even been known to rescue a human swimmer in distress. One woman, sucked under by a strong current and nearly dead, found herself being pushed upwards to the surface and then nudged towards the shore until she was safe. She was completely mystified, having no idea who was helping her in this way, but a witness later told her that he had clearly seen a dolphin carrying out the rescue.

Dolphins are intensely social animals. This is especially important in connection with their feeding behavior. They eat fish, but they rarely do this in a simple way, with one dolphin chasing after one fish. They prefer to act as cooperative fish-hunters. Hunting together gives them the chance to drive fish towards one another. Working as a team, they confuse the fish long enough to be able to snap them up.

Different groups of dolphins have different ways of confusing the fish. In one case it was found that they took turns in feasting. The whole group would surround a big shoal of fish and herd them together into a tight pack. Then one dolphin would swim through the mass of fish and eat its fill, while the others kept them surrounded. Then it would stop and let the next one eat as much as it could. This continued until each of the dolphins in the group had been given a chance to eat.

In some regions, dolphins have been known to help human fishermen with their catch in a similar way, driving shoals of fish into the men's nets. In other places, dolphins have been seen to use their high leaps out of the water as a way of spying on sea-birds. When sea-birds find a very large shoal of fish, a number of them gather there to catch their prey. Each time the dolphins jump clear of the water, their eyes quickly scan the ocean, looking for just such a cluster of sea-birds. When they spot the feeding birds, they swim at high speed to the spot and start their own hunting there.

After they have fed, the mood of the dolphins changes. Instead of becoming sleepy, like many other well-fed hunters, they become intensely playful. They keep swimming in and out of one another's groups, forever changing position, altering speed, and varying direction. They caress one another with their flippers. They swim belly-to-belly, or prod one another with their pointed snouts.

If a boat comes near they swim alongside it, riding on the bow-waves and leaping into the air time after time. Human swimmers sometimes find themselves being used as playthings. Snorkellers and divers may be teased by friendly dolphins that rush up behind them and knock their goggles off their faces.

Despite these occasional contacts with humans, nearly all their play takes place between one dolphin and another. This social playfulness has a special value. It makes sure that they get to know one another extremely well. They learn one another's moods and abilities. They find out how fast, how strong, how bright and how different each individual dolphin is. This helps them enormously when they are herding fish. The fish are so fast that it is vital for the dolphins to understand exactly how their friends and companions will act and react, how they will move and twist and dart through the water. Their lengthy playtimes, after bouts of feeding, give them this information.

Dolphins have a strange way of sending out signals. Being mammals rather than

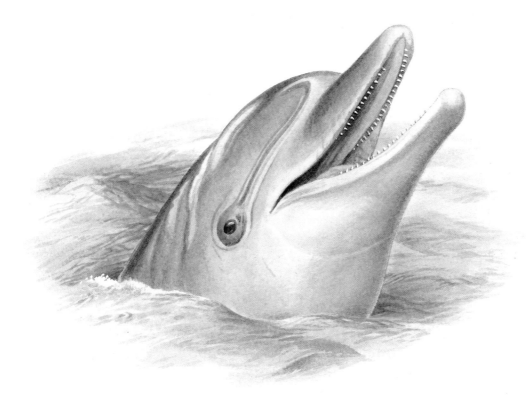

fish, they are quite noisy. Some fish grunt occasionally, but most are voiceless. Dolphins, on the other hand, produce a delightful variety of squeaks, chirps, trills and rattles. Certain of these sounds can be detected by the human ear, but the dolphin's range of hearing is so much greater than ours that many of its noises are completely inaudible to us. We only know that the animals are making these particular sounds because we can record them on special instruments.

Some people think that dolphins have a real language and that if, like Dr. Doolittle, we could learn their language, we could eventually start talking to them and discussing the important news of the day. Sadly, this is only a dream. They may have very big brains and they may make lots of strange noises, but they do not, if we are honest about it, have a true language. It is nice to think they do, but it is simply not the case.

They do, however, have a very special talent for using their noises to find their way about the oceans and to locate shoals of fish. This is a kind of sonar – an echo-location system. What happens is that the dolphin swims along, chirping and squeaking, and these very high-pitched sounds spread through the water until they hit some solid object. Then the sound-waves bounce back to the dolphin. The animal can tell how far away the object is by checking how long it takes for the sounds to return to its head. We use the same kind of sound detection in submarines, helping them to avoid collisions.

Part of the appeal of dolphins is the shape of their faces. Like humans they have a big, domed forehead (called a "melon forehead") and a mouth that turns up at the corners as if in a permanent smile. The dolphin is not smiling, of course, its mouth shape is completely fixed, but we react so strongly to smiling in our fellow humans that we simply cannot help but see the dolphin face as a smiling one. We therefore imagine that it is a cheerful, happy face and prefer to overlook the fact that even a dying dolphin or one in great pain would still have that fixed grin on its face. Any animal that can accidentally match pleasant human expressions, for whatever reason, is automatically much more popular with us than an animal that accidentally appears to be scowling or snarling.

With all its special qualities, it is easy to see why we find the dolphin so attractive. It wins on five counts: it has graceful movement, it is intelligent, it is helpful to those in trouble, it has a playful character and it has a face that always looks happy. These are all qualities we admire in human beings, so it is not surprising that we are so fond of the dolphin. No wonder it is one of the stars of the animal world.

Bearing in mind how extraordinary dolphins are, it comes as something of a shock to find that some countries kill and eat a huge number of them. The fishermen of Turkey, for example, kill more than 100,000 every year for food. Many people have become so attached to these animals that they find the idea of eating a dolphin steak quite repulsive. This is a measure of just how much we have all taken this delightful animal to our hearts in recent years, helped to a great extent by the television adventures of perhaps the most famous dolphin of all time . . . Flipper.

# The Kangaroo

WHEN CAPTAIN COOK WAS SAILING NEAR THE AUSTRALIAN CONTINENT IN 1770 he was shipwrecked on a coral reef and his ship badly damaged. While it was being repaired he and his companions explored the nearby mainland. There they saw an astounding animal leaping about on its hind legs and they asked the local people what it was. Not speaking English, the natives replied "Kangaroo" which meant "I don't understand you." Captain Cook thought they were telling him the name of the animal and, from that day to this, it has been called "kangaroo."

The explorers were surprised to see that these animals did not stand on four equal legs like other animals, but instead sat up on their big hind feet and carried their tiny front feet high up against their chests, like little hands. They noticed that each female had a pouch of skin, as if someone had added a large pocket in her coat of soft fur. The pouch was on the front of her body and in it she carried her baby. The faces of some of the young ones could be seen peering out of the tops of the pouches.

They were also fascinated by the way these animals moved. Watching carefully, they saw that when the kangaroos were feeding they advanced slowly by pushing themselves up on their short front legs and their powerful tail. In this position they swung their huge hind legs forward, then repeated the action. Using the tail in this way it was as if they had five legs instead of the usual four. With each stride they moved forward a distance of about 3 feet.

When alarmed, the kangaroos made a dramatic change. Now, neither the tail nor the front legs touched the ground. Instead the enormous hind feet stamped on the ground, throwing the animal forward in a huge bound. The body was balanced perfectly, so that the kangaroos could make leap after leap without pausing for rest. The front part of the body leant forward and its weight matched the heavy tail that stuck out stiffly behind.

The early explorers had never seen anything like it before, and marvelled at the speed of the kangaroos. They decided to test it. On their ship they had some hunting dogs which they had taken with them on their long voyage. These dogs were greyhounds and the explorers were sure that nothing could escape their high-speed sprinters. But they were wrong. When the greyhounds were let loose to chase the kangaroos, they failed to catch them. This was not because the dogs were slower, but because, when the kangaroos came to some tall grasses, they simply leapt over them and disappeared from the greyhounds' sight. The dogs did not know which way to go and lost their prey.

Its strange way of moving was not, however, to be the biggest surprise the kangaroo had in store. Later, when it was possible to study the animals more closely, it was discovered that the behavior of the baby kangaroo was even more extraordinary than that of its parents.

The young kangaroo takes only a month to form inside its mother's body. Then, when it is about to be born, the female spends two hours cleaning and licking the inside of her pouch. She sits herself up in a strange position, sometimes leaning against a tree, with her tail brought forward between her back legs. As soon as the baby is born it starts to crawl up the front of its mother's body, twisting from side to side in a snakelike movement as it climbs higher and higher. Finally, with a last great effort, it clambers into her wet pouch and safety. The whole, amazing journey takes about three minutes and is unaided by the mother.

The most remarkable fact about this tiny baby is the difference between its weight and that of its huge mother. It is hard to believe, but she can weigh 80,000 times as much as her newborn baby. The tiny creature is less than 1 inch long and weighs only about .03 of an ounce. It is blind and deaf, but it has a big nose with which it can smell its way around. Its skin is completely naked and, surprisingly, its front legs are bigger than its hind legs – just the opposite of the adult kangaroo. It makes good use of its strong front feet when dragging itself up through its mother's fur.

Once inside the pouch, the baby searches for a nipple and clamps on to it with its mouth. Inside its mouth the nipple swells up so much that the baby cannot be shaken loose even when, later on, the mother starts leaping about. It stays attached in this way for many weeks, feeding on her thin, watery milk, and growing bigger and bigger.

As time passes, the little kangaroo, or "joey," begins to stick its head out of the pouch and stares at the great world beyond its mother's body. When it is about six months old, it leaves the pouch for the first time and hops around on the ground near its mother. At this stage it never strays very far from her. At the first sign of any danger, it clambers back into the safety of the pouch.

When it is eight months old, it is too big to squeeze back inside the pouch, and must risk its chances in the outside world. If there is a sudden panic, it must hop alongside the adult kangaroos as best it can. But even at this late stage, it still wants to feed from its mother from time to time. Although it is eating grasses like the other members of the herd, it has not lost its thirst for its mother's milk.

Because the eight-month-old kangaroo is too big to climb into the pouch, it simply pushes its head inside and, standing on the ground in front of its mother, continues to feed from her nipple. At this age, though, she provides it with a different kind of milk, much thicker and richer than when it was very small. After about four months of feeding from outside the pouch like this, the young kangaroo is finally weaned. Even though it is now a year old, it is usually reluctant to leave its mother and keeps trying to nose into her pouch for just one more last feed. Eventually she has to drive it away, to start its own life and look after itself.

Less than one day after the big joey has left its mother's pouch, she gives birth to another baby, which immediately crawls up into the vacant space. At this point, she is providing two kinds of milk at once: the thin milk for the newborn from one nipple, and the thick, creamy milk for the big joey from another nipple.

The one-year-old kangaroo, no longer able to rely on help from its mother, must

now get all its food by grazing. Like the adults in the herd, it will be active only at night, munching away at the grasses in the long dark hours when it is cool, and then lying on its side in a patch of shade during the heat of the day. When it is resting it often makes a scooped-out bed for itself, a shallow dip in the ground that fits snugly around its heavy body.

When they get very hot, kangaroos cool themselves by panting like dogs, or by licking their fur. Once the fur is wet, the spittle acts like sweat and cools the animals as it is dried off by the sun. In some areas, they hop into caves during the heat of the day and stay there in the cool darkness for hours on end.

Kangaroos are bothered by many skin pests, but they have a special "comb" with which they can clean their fur and scratch themselves behind the ears. This comb is found on the hind foot, where the second and third toes are joined together, except at their tips. This gives them the ideal grooming tool, and helps to relieve them of at least some of the itchings caused by the insects that attack them.

Although grazing is the typical way of feeding for adult kangaroos, they can sometimes be seen browsing among small bushes. When they feed like this on leaves, they use their short front legs to pull the foliage towards their mouths.

Because they feed by night, kangaroos manage to obtain a lot of moisture from the grass, and they can go for a very long time without having to move to a water-hole or river to drink. In fact, they have been known to last for up to three months without water, which is much longer than most large mammals can manage.

There are two common kinds of large kangaroo, the red and the grey, and these are the biggest of all the pouched animals of Australia. The red kangaroo prefers to live on the open plains, while the grey one is found more often in the open forests.

There are also about fifty different kinds of smaller kangaroos, including tree kangaroos, rat kangaroos, wallaroos and wallabies. They nearly all live in Australia, but a few of them are found in Tasmania and New Guinea. Some are little bigger than rabbits, but they all have the same basic kangaroo shape.

The biggest male kangaroo ever found measured over 9 feet from the tip of its tail to its nose. The really large ones can be over 6 feet tall when sitting up on their hind feet and can leap 24 feet in a single bound. At the top of the leap they are more than 9 feet off the ground. When traveling at full speed they can move at 30 miles per hour. The biggest ones weigh 200 pounds.

When they defend themselves they rear back on their powerful tails, bring their huge hind feet up in the air and slash down with them in a quick, savage strike. This blow is strong enough to rip off a man's clothes and can even tear open the front of his body.

If two kangaroos are fighting one another, they use this same kicking action, grappling with their short front legs to gain a good position to deliver the winning blow. But before they start the fight, they always give plenty of warning. The huge males approach one another with a strange, stiff-legged walk, scratch their chests in an agitated way, and then pull themselves up to their full height, trying to look as impressive as possible. Only if these threats and displays fail to scare away the rival do the two animals set on one another and fight for real.

When chased by dogs, kangaroos will flee towards water if there is any nearby. Once there, they go in as deep as they can without losing their footing. Then, chest-deep, they turn and face their attackers. If the dogs swim up to them, the kangaroos grab them with their sharply-clawed hands and hold them under the water until they have drowned.

The only other enemies of kangaroos are eagles and pythons, which can attack young ones, and men with guns, who have slaughtered countless millions of these inoffensive creatures. One of the old excuses for killing them was that they competed with the newly imported sheep and other domestic stock for grazing land. Careful studies have since revealed that, in reality, kangaroos and domestic stock prefer different kinds of plant food and rarely compete seriously with one another.

Kangaroos have also been valued for their skins and their meat. In the early days, their meat was taken for human use, but today it is marketed mostly as pet food. So many are being killed that there is a risk that, one day, they may be lost from whole regions of the Australian continent. Already four kinds of the smaller kangaroos have become extinct since modern man arrived on the scene. The bigger ones are still common, it is true, but this does not mean they will always be safe. To many people, the kangaroo is the symbol of Australia, and it would be a tragedy if this amazing animal were to become yet another rarity in the twenty-first century.

# The Panda

THE GIANT PANDA IS THE GREATEST STAR OF THE ANIMAL WORLD. THE arrival of one of these appealing animals at a zoo always makes the headlines and the birth of a baby panda is world news. Crowds flock to gaze at it and everyone falls in love with it.

What is it that makes it so very popular? There are many reasons. First, it has an eye-catching black and white coat of fur. Its legs, shoulders, ears, eyes and the tip of its nose are all jet black. The rest of it is pure white. This black and white pattern is a favorite of human beings because it is so vivid. We know this is true because in the past we have always been so keen to breed black and white domestic animals from wild brown ones. We have black and white horses, dogs, goats, sheep, cattle, rabbits and even mice. So, when an animal like the panda comes along that is black and white already, without any help from us, we naturally find it very appealing.

Second, it is a giant. We have always been impressed by big animals and so the name "Giant Panda" makes it sound exciting, as though it is huge and strong – a friendly monster. The truth, though, is that it weighs no more than a human being. The reason it is called a giant is because its only living relative is the much smaller red panda. This little creature is no larger than a pet cat.

Third, it is very rare and comes from a strange, faraway land. Its wild home, in the bamboo forests of the mountains of China, is so difficult to visit that the panda has always been a mysterious creature, hardly ever seen in its natural habitat. This gives it a special kind of glamor, as though it is a famous film star that refuses to be interviewed.

The rarity of the giant panda also makes it tremendously valuable. If zoos want to buy one, they soon find that it will cost them more than any other animal. When Chi-Chi, one of the most famous of all giant pandas, was brought to London Zoo, the animal dealer who went to China to get her had to offer the Chinese a whole collection of other animals as a swap. The one, tiny panda cub cost him three giraffes, two rhinos, two hippos, and two zebras. He had to ship all of those to China, at great expense, just to be allowed to bring out his one small, but precious prize.

The shape of the panda also makes it popular. It has a flat face, which appeals to us because we too have flat faces. We like an animal that has "human" qualities. They make us feel more comfortable, as though they are old friends. Walt Disney has made great use of this when creating his animal "heroes." He gives friendly animals flat faces, while villains get long, pointed snouts.

When it is eating or resting, the panda often props itself up in a very human posture. If it is feeding on bamboo, it will hold the stem in one of its front feet and bring it up to its mouth. Many animals never do this, but the panda finds it easy. Any animal that can sit up straight has a special appeal for us because it reminds us of the way we ourselves do things.

The giant panda has a very short tail that can hardly be seen as it walks around. When the animal sits down, this little tail-stump becomes almost invisible. Again, because we humans have no tails, any animal that lacks a long tail is going to be more popular.

There are several ways in which the giant panda appears not only human, but babyish. It is round and soft, like a baby. It is also playful and clumsy like a little toddler. And the black markings on its face make it look very big-eyed when seen from a distance. This also reminds us of the human infant.

Being babyish in these ways helps to increase the giant panda's appeal. It makes us feel protective towards the animal. We want to cuddle and pet it. When we are young, we do this with our toy pandas and before long we start thinking that even adult pandas must be harmless, big, soft furry friends, too. So we are amazed to discover that, in real life, when fully grown they can become dangerous and even violent. One giant panda in an American zoo attacked his keeper so badly that he lost an arm.

Even the much loved Chi-Chi at London Zoo suddenly turned savage one day. Without any warning she knocked her sixteen-year-old keeper to the ground and sat on him. They had often enjoyed rough-and-tumble play together in the past when she had been a little cub, but she was now fully grown and her mood had changed. She was not playing any more. As the boy lay helpless on the ground, pinned beneath her heavy body, she attacked his right leg with her powerful jaws. Blood was pouring from his leg and he started screaming for help. Another keeper leapt into the panda's paddock and rescued him, but the boy was so seriously injured that he was not able to return to work for seven months. The day he came back, Chi-Chi saw him and started growling ferociously at him. For his own safety he was never allowed to enter her enclosure again.

This boy had become very fond of Chi-Chi and had never done anything to annoy her, so her savage behavior came as a great shock. What had caused it? In the years since the attack we have learned much more about the way pandas live in China and we think we understand them a little better. We now know that wild pandas want to be completely alone as soon as they become fully grown. So Chi-Chi had probably decided, one morning, that the time had come to say goodbye to her old friend. Most animals would only have threatened to attack and made their feelings plain without drawing blood. But Chi-Chi was much more violent.

The reason we find this so surprising is because of the panda's special appeal – all those human and "babyish" features it has, which make it look so cuddly. It goes to prove that we must always try to understand an animal from its own point of view, and not from ours. Just because an animal looks friendly, does not mean that it *is* friendly. In the same way, just because some other animal looks fierce does not mean that it is. Appearances can be misleading in the world of animals. Some of the nastiest-looking animals are easy to handle and some of the nicest-looking ones, like the giant pandas, can become really vicious.

It would be wrong to blame Chi-Chi for her attack. It was not her fault. All she was doing was saying, in a brutal way, I have reached the age where I want to have my own private territory and I will not share it with anyone. From her point of view this was a perfectly natural thing to do. We simply did not understand her well enough.

One vital clue may have been missed. Because we found the black and white design of the panda's furry coat so attractive, we did not stop to ask why the animal should have markings of this kind. There is a lesson to be learned here from another black and white animal – the skunk.

Although much smaller than the giant panda, the skunk has very similar markings when seen from a distance. In the case of the skunk we know that this coat pattern acts as a warning to enemies. Skunks can squirt a stinking liquid at their attackers which stings their eyes and leaves them with a disgusting smell sprayed all over them. The stink does not leave them for days and, rather naturally, they never forget their first encounter with a skunk. The way they remember the animal, so that they can recognize it if they meet it again, is by its very unusual black and white markings. This warning pattern becomes the skunk's "flag," saying "I am dangerous, keep away!"

Bearing this in mind, it seems sensible to think of the giant panda's markings as being another warning signal. But the panda cannot squirt a stinking spray over its enemies, so what is it warning them about? What is its secret weapon?

To find the answer we must take a look at the way the animal feeds. Millions of years ago, the ancestors of the giant panda were once meat-eaters, but as the centuries passed, they became more and more fond of vegetable foods. They still ate a little meat from time to time, but most of their meals now came from plants. In particular they chewed the tough shoots of the bamboos that they found growing in huge numbers in their mountain homes. These shoots were not easy to crunch up and the jaws of the pandas became bigger and stronger. They became so strong that, if attacked by natural enemies such as wild dogs, they could defend themselves with ease, snapping a dog's leg as easily as a hard stick of bamboo.

The giant panda's new weapon, then, was its amazingly powerful bite, and it needed to advertise this to other animals. It wanted to say "Do not even bother to try biting me, because I can crunch you into little pieces." If it could send out a signal saying this, it could prevent attacks from starting and would be able to enjoy a much more peaceful way of life.

The original pandas probably had dull brown coats, like most other mammals, but as millions of years passed, the dull brown changed gradually into the vivid black and white. Now the pandas could show themselves to their enemies from a distance, like the skunks. Bloodthirsty battles could be avoided. Young attackers, meeting pandas for the first time and making a mistake, could remember them much more easily and avoid them in future. Just as the panda-boy at London Zoo never again went near Chi-Chi, so the wild dogs and leopards would never try twice to get near a wild giant panda.

Because adult pandas live alone in the wild, they have a very short breeding season, the males and females coming together only for mating, and then going their separate ways once more. Eventually, on her own, the female gives birth to her tiny, rat-sized baby in the safety of a hollow tree, or in some simple den or lair. At birth the infant weighs no more than 5 ounces. Its mother weighs eight hundred times as much.

The newborn panda is blind and toothless and spends most of its time cradled in its mother's arms. She sits up to do this, looking very much like a human mother as she cuddles and fondles her new arrival. The baby can crawl when it is about three months old. It grows quickly and puts on weight at an amazing rate. The mother remains very protective and watches over her infant with great care and tenderness. As soon as it starts to become adult, however, all this changes and the youngster will have to set off by itself to find its own, private feeding grounds, regardless of whether it is a male or a female. The solo lifestyle of the giant panda will then take over and, except for the brief mating seasons each year, this extraordinary animal will pass its days alone in the vast bamboo forests.

Tragically, there are less than a thousand giant pandas left alive today. Some people think that, in the entire world, there may be no more than six or seven hundred of them. The Chinese have realized how valuable they are and are doing their best to stop the numbers getting any smaller, but this is not easy. Despite all their efforts to protect the pandas, it is feared that they may all finally vanish during the next century.

The main danger they face is that their bamboo forests are slowly being chopped down by people needing more farming land. Another risk comes from accidental trapping. Although the pandas themselves are not hunted, snares that are set for other animals sometimes catch them and cause their deaths.

In addition, there are a few smugglers who are deliberately killing giant pandas, even today, for their skins. These are secretly taken out of the country and sold to rich foreigners who are prepared to pay up to $200,000 for a single black and white panda-skin. Desperate to stop this, the Chinese have now increased the punishment for skin-trading from life imprisonment to death. Some smugglers have already been executed. But despite everyone's efforts the truth is that the giant panda will probably be the first of the world's great animal stars to vanish in the near future.